100 MUST-READ
LIFE-CHANGING
BOOKS

Nick Rennison

A & C Black • London

First published 2008
A & C Black Publishers Limited
36 Soho Square
London W1D 3QY
www.acblack.com

© 2008 Nick Rennison

ISBN: 978-0-7136-8872-6

A CIP catalogue record for this book is available from
the British Library.

This book is produced using paper that is made from wood grown in
managed, sustainable forests. It is natural, renewable and recyclable.
The logging and manufacturing processes conform to the environmental
regulations of the country of origin.

Typeset in 8.5pt on 12pt Meta-Light

Printed and bound in Great Britain by
CPI Bookmarque, Croydon, CR0 4TD

CONTENTS

ABOUTTHISBOOK

The individual entries in the guide are arranged A to Z by author. They describe the chosen books as concisely as possible and say something briefly about the writer and his or her life. Each entry is followed by a 'Read on' list which includes books by the same author, books by similar authors or books on a theme relevant to the entry. Scattered throughout the text there are also 'Read on a theme' menus which list between six and a dozen titles united by a common theme.

All the first choice books in this guide have dates attached to them. In the case of English and American writers, there is one date which indicates first publication in the UK or the USA. For translated writers, there are two dates. The first indicates publication in the original language and the second is the date of the book's first appearance in English. For example, Simone de Beauvoir's *The Second Sex* is marked as 1949 (first publication in French) and 1953 (first translation into English). For some older texts, either there is no commonly accepted date for publication or the idea of publication, in the modern sense, was largely meaningless in the social context in which they were written. In these instances, approximate dates for the writing of the texts have been given.

In choosing the 100 books for this guide, I have followed in the footsteps of *Desert Island Discs*. The guests on that long-running radio programme are always asked about the one book that they would take with them to the desert island but it is assumed that the Bible and the Complete Works of Shakespeare are already awaiting them on the sands beneath the palm trees. In the same way, I have excluded the Bible, the Koran and other major religious texts as well as Shakespeare from my list. On the basis that poetry is too large a subject to have what could be seen as just a token presence in this guide, I have also omitted volumes of verse. Khalil Gibran's *The Prophet*, which some people would label poetry, I *have* included because I prefer to categorise it as lyrical prose.

INTRODUCTION

What exactly is a 'life-changing' book? There is no genre of 'life-changing' literature in the same sense that there are genres of 'crime fiction', 'romantic fiction' and 'science fiction' yet nearly all enthusiastic readers would acknowledge that some books they have read have had a profound impact on them. Books that change lives undoubtedly exist. This guide is not meant to provide a list of the 'best' life-changing books available. The idea that there can be a definitive list of the books most likely to change lives, and change them for the better, is a ludicrous one. Books *can* change lives but they do so in a wide variety of often subtle ways. Very different books can, in different ways, be life-changing and the selection of titles in this book reflects that. *100 Must-Read Life-Changing Books* finds space for, amongst others, a children's novel about a young girl who discovers a key to a secret garden, a Chinese text on war from the sixth century BC, a black comedy set in the Second World War, the autobiography of one of the twentieth century's most remarkable statesmen, a handbook on happiness by one of the world's great religious leaders and a fable about a pilot who meets a story-telling child in the Sahara desert. What such widely varying books *do* have in common is that they have all changed the lives of readers in the past and they will continue to do so in the future.

Some books can change people in very specific ways. Those oppressed by racism can take strength from works like the autobiographies of

Nelson Mandela and Malcolm X. Women can reassess society and their own position in it after reading books like *The Female Eunuch* or *The Beauty Myth*. Those who feel themselves alienated from the world can take heart from reading about the lives of those, like Helen Keller, who have triumphed over the most extraordinary odds. This guide includes a significant number of titles which fall into this category.

Other books have a greater life-changing impact when read at one age than they do when read at another. Some novels read in adolescence (Salinger's *The Catcher in the Rye*, for example, or Kerouac's *On the Road*) can fundamentally alter the way in which the reader views the world. They become so identified with a particular period in the reader's life that re-reading them later can be a disconcerting, even disillusioning, experience. Yet adolescence is not the only age at which certain books are likely to have their most profound effect. E.M. Forster once wrote that, 'the only books that influence us are those for which we are ready, and which have gone a little farther down our particular path than we have yet got ourselves'. And, as Doris Lessing says in her introduction to a 1971 edition of her novel *The Golden Notebook* (a book which has its own place in this guide), 'Remember that the book which bores you when you are twenty or thirty will open doors for you when you are forty or fifty — and vice versa.' Her advice to readers ('Don't read a book out of its right time for you') remains valid.

Books that make us look at the world anew can be either fiction or non-fiction. Both have their place in a guide to life-changing literature. Novels can be much more than just entertainment – engaging narratives with which to while away some of life's idler moments. Very often emotional truths can be better conveyed through stories than they can by any other means. The stories we have always told ourselves give meaning to our lives and help to draw us out of the narrow sphere of self into a more active engagement with others. It should come as no surprise to learn that about a third of the titles in *100 Must-Read Life-Changing Books* will be found on the Fiction shelves in any bookshop or library.

The two-thirds of titles in the guide that are non-fiction can be further sub-divided into a number of smaller categories. There are memoirs of remarkable people which can inspire new ways of seeing our own lives. There are masterpieces of spiritual insight, which can re-adjust one's sense of the human and the divine and the relationship between them, and books by distinguished scientists which explain for non-scientists the often dizzying ideas about the nature of the universe and about ourselves which modern physics and biology have revealed. Other entries in the guide introduce the works of psychologists whose writings re-interpret human nature, self-help authors who can open up new paths through life for people in trouble and commentators whose wisdom and understanding make us look again at the kind of society we have created.

I have tried to make the selection of 100 books in this guide as interesting and varied as I could. Some were written more than 2,000 years ago, some in the last 20 years. Some present a simple and direct message to their readers, others a demanding and challenging intellectual argument. Some are the work of people who are household names, others by writers who are less well-known than, perhaps, they should be. There were titles which it was very difficult to ignore. It would be difficult to argue with the sheer statistics of numbers of copies sold and claim that books like Paulo Coelho's *The Alchemist* and Richard Bach's *Jonathan Livingston Seagull* do not deserve their places in a guide to life-changing books. There are other titles (Jean Giono's *The Man Who Planted Trees*, for example) which may not have quite the fame that others do but which, I would argue, have a message for readers just as important.

There is sometimes an assumption that, if we want to change our lives for the better, the books that we read should be relentlessly upbeat and optimistic. It is an assumption on which many a career in writing self-help and business books has been built but it is, I think, a false one. We cannot change ourselves or our lives in any meaningful way by pretending that the world is other than it is or that terrible things do not happen in it. A significant number of the books in this guide have as their subject matter some of the worst events in human history. Yet, paradoxically, books about the Holocaust (Primo Levi's *If This Is a Man* or Elie Wiesel's *Night*) or Stalinist terror (Nadezhda Mandelstam's *Hope Against Hope*) can be the ones which alter readers' views of life the most. Perhaps it is only through facing up to the suffering and wretchedness in the world that people can come to appreciate the best that it has to offer.

I return to the point I made in the first paragraph of this introduction. Books that change lives inarguably exist. I believe that every single one of the 100 titles I have chosen for this guide can be placed in the category of 'life-changing' books. However, the ways in which books change lives are multifarious and the titles in *100 Must-Read Life-Changing Books* have been selected in order to reflect this fact. Any reading guide which includes books by J.K. Rowling and Germaine Greer, Richard Dawkins and Mahatma Gandhi, Stephen Hawking and J.R.R. Tolkien is going to be wide-ranging, whatever else it is. I hope that it will also prove inspirational enough to send readers off in search of books that they might not otherwise have read. And – who knows? – perhaps some of those readers will find their lives changed.

A–Z LIST OF ENTRIES BY AUTHOR

The following is a checklist of authors featured in this book.

A–ZOFENTRIES

ISABEL ALLENDE (b. 1942) PERU/CHILE

THE HOUSE OF THE SPIRITS (1982)

Isabel Allende was born in Peru, where her father was Chilean ambassador, and had a peripatetic upbringing around the world as the family moved from country to country. As a young woman she worked for a time in Europe but she was living in Chile in 1973 when the coup which brought to an end the democratic government of her cousin Salvador Allende put her life in danger and she was forced into exile. Her first novel for adults, *The House of the Spirits*, became an international bestseller and she has since published more than a dozen further books, both fiction and non-fiction. 'What I don't write, I forget,' Isabel Allende once said, 'and then it is as if it never happened; by writing about my life I can live twice.' Allende has always drawn heavily on her own life in her writing. Even her fiction, so often hailed as the embodiment of 'magic realism' and so filled with imagination and invention, often has its roots in the story of her family. In *The House of the Spirits* strange and wonderful things may happen but, at its heart, it is a family saga of love and life and death. Three generations of women provide the backbone of the story, from the moment when the clairvoyant Clara del Valle first sees her future to the terrible events which circle around her granddaughter Alba.

The book was only the first of Isabel Allende's remarkable works of fiction which have ranged from *Of Love and Shadows*, a novel in which the brutal politics of South America and magic realism meet and mingle, to *Zorro*, her own very particular take on the legend of the swashbuckling, masked hero. By living twice in her own writing, Isabel Allende has provided her readers with some memorable experiences.

🍃**Read on**

Of Love and Shadows, Paula

Gabriel Garcia Marquez, *Love in the Time of Cholera*; Alice Walker, *The Temple of My Familiar*

MAYA ANGELOU (b. 1928) USA

I KNOW WHY THE CAGED BIRD SINGS (1970)

As a young woman, Maya Angelou was a singer and actress, touring the world in Gershwin's *Porgy and Bess* and working in New York nightclubs. In the 1960s she became a civil rights activist and spent five years in Africa as a journalist and teacher. Today she is one of America's most respected poets and writers. Her finest work is the reconstruction of her own life she has made in several volumes of autobiography. The first of these is *I Know Why the Caged Bird Sings* which records the difficulties of her upbringing in the American Deep South during the 1930s. With her brother, the young Maya is sent to live with her grandmother who runs a store in a small town in Arkansas. She learns much from her grandmother but she also witnesses the endemic racism in the town and the casual contempt that the white people have for the black. Still only eight years old, Maya is then despatched to stay with her mother in St. Louis where she is raped by her mother's current boyfriend. Mute with trauma and distress, the girl withdraws into her shell and few people other than her brother are able to reach her. In her adolescence, and now living permanently with her mother in San Francisco, Maya continues to suffer guilt and misery. She becomes pregnant while still at high school and the first volume of the autobiography ends with the birth of her child and her realisation that new responsibilities demand a new commitment to life. Poignantly recreating Maya Angelou's struggle to forge her own identity and to triumph over the obstacles of being black and poor in a racist society, *I Know Why the Caged Bird Sings* repays reading and re-reading. It is a scathing indictment of injustice yet it also holds out hope that even the worst of circumstances can be left behind.

⪢Read on

Gather Together in My Name; *Singin' and Swingin' and Gettin' Merry Like Christmas*; *The Heart of a Woman*; *All God's Children Need Traveling Shoes* (the other volumes of autobiography)
Zora Neale Hurston, *Dust Tracks on a Road*

MARGARET ATWOOD (b. 1939) CANADA

THE HANDMAID'S TALE (1985)

Margaret Atwood is one of Canada's most admired living writers and her works range from volumes of prize-winning poetry to historical fiction like *Alias Grace*, the story of an enigmatic nineteenth century serving maid who may or may not be a murderess, and novels (*The Edible Woman*, for example) which explore questions of gender and identity. Probably her finest books, however, use motifs and ideas from science fiction to throw new light on contemporary debates about feminism and the position of women. Of these books the most interesting remains *The Handmaid's Tale*. The novel is set in the near future in the Republic of Gilead, where fundamentalist Christianity rules and the laws are those of Genesis. Women are chattels: they have no identity, no privacy and no happiness except what men permit them. Offred, for example, is a Handmaid, and her life is devoted to one duty only: breeding. In Gilead public prayers and hangings are the norm; individuality – even looking openly into a man's face or reading a woman's magazine – is punished by mutilation, banishment or death. Atwood shows Offred's struggle to keep her sanity and her identity in such a situation, and her equivocal relationship with the feminist Underground which may be Gilead's only hope. Through the dystopian prism of Gilead, Atwood is able to investigate many of the issues of gender and sexuality which trouble our own society and to suggest that forces in contemporary society (religious fundamentalism, anti-feminism) could only too easily accommodate the worst forms of totalitarianism. With great imaginative power she takes some of the darker possibilities of sexual politics and draws them out to extreme but entirely logical conclusions. *The Handmaid's Tale* is a memorable novel which uses a fictional future to ring warning bells for today.

See also: *100 Must-Read Science Fiction Novels*

≋Read on
The Edible Woman; *Oryx and Crake*
Angela Carter, *The Passion of New Eve*; P.D. James, *The Children of Men*; Marge Piercy, *Woman on the Edge of Time*; Joanna Russ, *The Female Man*

MARCUS AURELIUS (121–180 AD) ITALY

MEDITATIONS (c. 170–180)
Roman emperors are remembered for many things – military triumphs, great buildings which bear their names, indulgence in fabulously decadent pleasures – but not usually for their philosophical insights. The exception to the rule that emperors were not profound thinkers was Marcus Aurelius, who ruled the far-flung empire from 161 AD to his death nearly twenty years later. His thoughts have come down to us in the shape of the 12 books of his *Meditations*, originally written in Greek (to Romans, the language of philosophy) and put together over a ten-year period whilst he was on military campaigns in Eastern Europe. These reflect the influence of the ancient philosophical tradition known as

Stoicism (although Marcus Aurelius never specifically describes himself as a Stoic) and of the Greek philosopher Epictetus in particular. A Stoic believed that the wise man was indifferent to the external world. Virtue rather than health or wealth or power was the great good in life and the attainment of virtue was a matter of the individual will. A man could be virtuous when sick, virtuous when poor, virtuous even (like Socrates) when under threat of death. What he needed to do was to cultivate the reason, to recognise the inevitable realities of the world and to turn his back on the destructive power of irrationality and the emotions. In some ways the philosophy Marcus Aurelius espoused can seem a bleak one, emphasising the difficulty of life and duty, but it can also be a liberating one in as much as it champions the mind's power over external circumstance. Through rigorous training the mind can be shaped and the character changed for the better. 'Such as are your habitual thoughts,' the emperor wrote, 'such also will be the character of your mind; for the soul is dyed by the thoughts.'

⮧Read on

Boethius, *The Consolation of Philosophy*; Cicero, *On the Good Life*; Epictetus, *The Discourses*; Seneca, *Letters from a Stoic*

RICHARD BACH (b. 1936) USA

JONATHAN LIVINGSTON SEAGULL (1970)

Who would have thought that a slim fable in which a seagull discovers the truths about life and flight would become one of the bestselling books of the 1970s? Richard Bach had already served as a pilot in the US Air Force and had written a number of books about flying and aircraft when he hit the bestselling jackpot with *Jonathan Livingston Seagull*. Bach's brief text, accompanied by Russell Munson's photographs of seagulls in flight, caught the public's imagination and the book went on to sell millions. It focuses on the experiences of one bird – the gull of the title – who dreams of flying faster and more freely than the other birds in the flock. Eventually he succeeds in reaching at least some of his goals but he is appalled to discover that the other gulls do not applaud his achievements. Instead he is told that his desire for faster and better ways of flying is unwelcome and he is banished from the flock. It is only when he is introduced to an elite band of gulls who, like him, have broken free of the limits that the ordinary birds have imposed upon themselves that he can reach his full potential. Heaven is on the horizon for him. As one of the elite gulls tells him, 'You will begin to touch heaven, Jonathan, in the moment that you touch perfect speed. And that isn't flying a thousand miles an hour, or a million, or flying at the speed of light. Because any number is a limit, and perfection doesn't have limits. Perfect speed, my son, is being there.' Richard Bach's allegorical example of 'New Age' spirituality is an easy read but more profound thoughts about the possible consequences of casting off tired routines and ways of thinking lurk behind its simplicity.

≋**Read on**

Illusions; *The Bridge Across Forever*

Paul Gallico, *The Snow Goose*; Oriah Mountain Dreamer, *The Invitation*

FRANCES HODGSON BURNETT (1849–1924)
UK/USA

THE SECRET GARDEN (1909)

Born in Manchester, Frances Hodgson moved with her family to Knoxville, Tennessee when she was in her teens. She married Dr Swan Burnett and moved with him to Washington DC in 1873. Her stories had begun to appear in American magazines in the late 1860s and her first novel, a tale of life in the Lancashire she had left behind, was published in 1877. During her lifetime, she was most famous for her novel *Little Lord Fauntleroy*, the sentimental story of a young American boy of cloying goodness and innocence who is summoned back to his father's native land, England, to be trained to take his place among the landed gentry. *Little Lord Fauntleroy*, both the book and the character, are a little too saccharine for today's tastes but another of Burnett's novels, published much later in her life, has deservedly retained its popularity and its appeal. *The Secret Garden* has its share of the same sentimentality that sometimes mars Burnett's other fiction but the story of the orphan Mary Lennox, whose misery when she is despatched to her uncle's gloomy house on the Yorkshire Moors is only relieved by her discovery of a mysterious walled garden, has a magic all its own. As

Mary tends the garden, she is able to share it with two other children in the house – Dickon, the green-fingered servant boy who helps her to bring it to life, and Colin, the sickly cousin who is transformed by his experiences in it. Few other books written for a younger readership convey so well both to children and to the adults they become that private delight that Mary has when 'she was inside the wonderful garden, and she could come through the door under the ivy any time, and she felt she had found a world all her own'. Mary Lennox's secret garden is a place that changes those who visit it; the novel to which it gives a title also changes lives.

🕮Read on

A Little Princess
Edith Nesbit, *Five Children and It*; Philippa Pearce, *Tom's Midnight Garden*

READ ON A THEME: CLASSICS FOR CHILDREN (AND ADULTS)

L. Frank Baum, *The Wonderful Wizard of Oz*
Roald Dahl, *Charlie and the Chocolate Factory*
Kenneth Grahame, *The Wind in the Willows*
Charles Kingsley, *The Water Babies*
Rudyard Kipling, *The Jungle Book*
C.S. Lewis, *The Lion, the Witch and the Wardrobe*

A.A. Milne, *Winnie the Pooh*
L.M. Montgomery, *Anne of Green Gables*
Edith Nesbit, *The Railway Children*
Anna Sewell, *Black Beauty*
Noel Streatfeild, *Ballet Shoes*
E.B. White, *Charlotte's Web*

JOSEPH CAMPBELL (1904–87) USA

THE HERO WITH A THOUSAND FACES (1949)

Joseph Campbell was a graduate student at Columbia University in the 1920s when he realised that many of the themes and motifs of the Arthurian literature he was studying were similar to those of the North American Indian folklore he had read and heard about when he was a child. It was a revelation to him and it was an insight that was to be at the heart of all his later work. As he wrote in his seminal work of comparative mythology *The Hero with a Thousand Faces*, 'There are of course differences between the numerous mythologies and religions of mankind, but this is a book about similarities; and once they are understood the differences will be found to be much less great than is popularly (and politically) supposed.' Central to so many of the world's great mythologies, Campbell argues, is the story of the hero and a journey he makes that transforms him. From his quiet life at home, the hero is called to action and must set off into the unknown in quest of his own particular grail. After a series of lesser trials en route to his goal he must then face a supreme challenge. If he passes this, he is able to take home the knowledge he has gained in his travels. The impact of Campbell's ideas on the arts has been immense. The film-maker George Lucas famously cited Campbell's work as an influence but it is not just *Star Wars* that owes him a debt. Plenty of other creative individuals – musicians, poets and visual artists – have found inspiration in his ideas. And the idea of the hero and his testing odyssey carries echoes of the journey we all make from birth to death. In Campbell's eyes, we can all be the heroes of our own lives if we choose to be.

≷Read on

Myths to Live By; *The Hero's Journey*
Bruno Bettelheim, *The Uses of Enchantment*; Sir James Frazier, *The Golden Bough*; Marina Warner, *From the Beast to the Blonde*

ALBERT CAMUS (1913–60) ALGERIA/FRANCE

THE REBEL (1951/1953)
Born in Algeria, Camus became a leading figure in French literary life during the Second World War with the publication of his novel *The Outsider* and his philosophical essay *The Myth of Sisyphus*. In the decade after the war he gained an international reputation and he was awarded the Nobel Prize for literature in 1957, three years before he was

killed in a car crash. Throughout his relatively short life, in newspaper articles, plays, essays and novels, Camus explored the position of what he called *l'homme révolté*, the rebel or misfit who feels out of tune with the spirit of the times. From Meursault in *The Outsider* to Dr Rieux in *The Plague*, the man who refuses to conform to the standard values of his society is at the heart of his fiction. In *The Rebel*, Camus wrote a book-length essay about *l'homme révolté* which examines the motives behind the urge to rebel, the nature of revolution and the mingled dangers and opportunities it offers. Camus is unequivocal about the importance of the rebel, the person who stands against 'the world of master and slave' and thus proves that 'there is something more in history than the relation between mastery and servitude' and that 'unlimited power is not the only law'. However, he is also clear-sighted enough to realise that successful rebels or revolutionaries can be corrupted by the power that they seize through their rebellion and that, as history shows only too often, a revolutionary government can easily become more despotic than the regime it replaced. Drawing on a wide range of writers and thinkers, from the Marquis de Sade to Karl Marx, Camus creates a very individual argument about the importance of the rebel and a spirited defence of his assertion that, 'It is those who know how to rebel, at the appropriate moment, against history who really advance its interests.'

See also: *100 Must-Read Classic Novels*

❧Read on
The Myth of Sisyphus; *The Outsider*
Jean-Paul Sartre, *Nausea*

FRITJOF CAPRA (b. 1939) AUSTRIA/USA

THE TURNING POINT (1982)

An academic physicist with a long-standing interest in Taoism, Zen Buddhism and other Eastern religions, Fritjof Capra attempted to marry his scientific and religious interests in his 1975 book *The Tao of Physics*. He was struck by the similarities between the world revealed by cutting-edge science and the world revealed by the religions of the East, noting that he was often encountering 'statements where it is almost impossible to say whether they have been made by physicists or by Eastern mystics'. Seven years later, Capra published *The Turning Point* in which he expanded his focus beyond the revolution in modern physics to examine ways in which science and philosophy are moving away from a mechanistic view of nature and towards a more holistic one. Just as physicists have been obliged over the course of the twentieth century to abandon many of their most cherished ideas about the nature of reality, so too will people working in fields as different as ecology and psychology, biology and economics, need to leave behind reductionist models of how the world works. And the rest of us will have to be prepared to accept a new vision of reality. In place of the old and tired models, Capra advocates 'a perception of reality that goes beyond the scientific framework to an intuitive awareness of the oneness of all life, the interdependence of its multiple manifestations and its cycles of change and transformation.' The consequences if we make the wrong decisions at 'the turning point' will be catastrophic. We are facing 'a crisis of a scale and urgency unprecedented in recorded human history' and outmoded ways of thinking cannot deal with it. *The Turning Point* was first published a quarter of a century ago and some of its arguments may now seem outmoded themselves but its central message about the importance of a holistic vision of life is even more valid than it once was.

🕮Read on

The Tao of Physics; *Uncommon Wisdom*; *The Web of Life*
Gregory Bateson, *Mind and Nature*; Ilya Prigogine and Isabelle Stengers, *Order Out of Chaos*

READONATHEME: NEW PHYSICS, NEW PHILOSOPHY

David Bohm, *Wholeness and the Implicate Order*
Paul Davies, *The Mind of God*
David Deutsch, *The Fabric of Reality*
Werner Heisenberg, *Physics and Philosophy*
F. David Peat, *Blackfoot Physics*
Michael Talbot, *The Holographic Universe*
Frank J. Tipler, *The Physics of Immortality*
Fred Alan Wolf, *The Spiritual Universe*
Gary Zukav, *The Dancing Wu Li Masters*

RACHEL CARSON (1907–64) USA

SILENT SPRING (1962)

'The earth's vegetation,' Rachel Carson wrote in her 1960s bestseller *Silent Spring*, 'is part of a web of life in which there are intimate and essential relations between plants and animals. Sometimes we have no choice but to disturb these relationships, but we should do so thoughtfully, with full awareness that what we do may have consequences remote in time and place.' Today, the thought she expressed is not an unusual one but she was one of the first people to bring such thinking to the attention of a wide public. Carson, born on a small farm in Pennsylvania, grew up to work as a marine biologist for the US Bureau of Fisheries. Her talents as a popular science writer were first displayed in books like *The Sea Around Us* (1951) and *The Edge of the Sea* (1955). The success of these earlier books, widely praised for their combination of rigorous science and an elegant, lyrical prose style, enabled her to become a full-time writer and it was then that she began the research into the pollution of the environment which eventually resulted in *Silent Spring*. The specific target of the book was the irresponsible use of pesticides but Carson's more general aim was to highlight the powerful and usually negative impact of human beings on the natural world. A pioneer of the environmental movement, Rachel Carson was one of the first people to realise the damage we were doing to the web of life of which she wrote and, as such, she deserves to be remembered and honoured. Her profound belief that, 'the more clearly we can focus our attention on the wonders and realities of the universe about us, the less taste we shall have for destruction' remains an inspiration more than forty years after her premature death.

≋Read on

The Edge of the Sea; *The Sea Around Us*
Annie Dillard, *Pilgrim at Tinker Creek*; Loren Eiseley, *The Immense Journey*

READ ON A THEME: IN TOUCH WITH NATURE

James Hamilton-Paterson, *Seven Tenths*
W.H. Hudson, *Green Mansions*
Barry Lopez, *Arctic Dreams*
Peter Matthiessen, *The Snow Leopard*
Gavin Maxwell, *Ring of Bright Water*
John Muir, *The Mountains of California*
John Stewart Collis, *The Worm Forgives the Plough*
Gilbert White, *The Natural History of Selborne*
Henry Williamson, *Tarka the Otter*

CARLOS CASTANEDA (1925–98) PERU/USA

THE TEACHINGS OF DON JUAN (1968)

Carlos Castaneda was an anthropology student at UCLA for much of the 1960s and his first published writings supposedly grew out of field work he undertook as part of his studies. His books have always been controversial. They purport to record his travels in the desert regions of the southwest United States and Mexico and his training, under the guidance of a Yaqui Indian he calls Don Juan, in the techniques of shamanism. Many have doubted the reality of Castaneda's Indian guru and have questioned the teachings he allegedly passed on. Whatever the truth about the existence or non-existence of Don Juan and about the content of Castaneda's books, there can be no doubt about the popularity of his writings. People responded in the sixties and seventies to his message and they continue to do so. At the heart of this message is the demand that we forget what we think we know about reality. There is a different order of reality hidden behind the everyday world we usually inhabit and those with courage can reach it. By means of initiation rituals, training and psychedelic drugs, Don Juan endeavours to show his disciple this 'separate reality'. It is there to be experienced if only we are prepared to rid ourselves of our egotism and self-important belief that we are at the centre of things. We are like horses with blinkers but our blinkers can be removed. 'For me there is only the travelling on paths that have heart,' Don Juan tells Castaneda, 'on any path that may have heart. There I travel, and the only worthwhile challenge is to traverse its full length. And there I travel, looking, looking breathlessly.' Through Castaneda's writings the old shaman invites those prepared to abandon conventional thinking to join him.

See also: *100 Must-Read Books for Men*

⮂Read on

A Separate Reality; *Journey to Ixtlan*
Taisha Abelar, *The Sorcerers' Crossing*; Don Miguel Ruiz, *The Four Agreements*; Victor Sanchez, *The Teachings of Don Carlos*

READ ON A THEME: NATIVE WISDOM

Black Elk, *Black Elk Speaks*
Charles Eastman, *The Soul of the Indian*
Joan Halifax, *Shamanic Voices*
Michael Harner, *The Way of the Shaman*
Sun Bear, *The Medicine Wheel*
Hank Wesselman, *Spiritwalker*

JUNG CHANG (b. 1952) CHINA/UK

WILD SWANS (1992)

Jung Chang was born into the new China ruled by Chairman Mao (about whom she was later to write a highly critical biography) and she grew up in comparatively privileged circumstances as the daughter of two leading Communist Party officials. She became a youthful Red Guard during the Cultural Revolution but, as she witnessed the violence and the public humiliation of many teachers and officials (including her own parents) that it encouraged, she grew rapidly disillusioned with its supposed progress. In 1978, after the political rehabilitation of her father, she became one of the few students from the People's Republic to be allowed to attend a university in Britain and, although she has returned regularly to her native country, she has lived in the West since then. *Wild Swans* was published in 1992 and became a worldwide bestseller. In her book Jung Chang brilliantly and vividly captures the history of China in the 20th century through stories of the lives of three women – her grandmother, her mother and herself. All three experienced terrible upheaval and human suffering. Jung Chang's grandmother was sold as a concubine to a warlord during the years of chaos that followed the collapse of the Manchu Empire; her mother lived through the turmoil of the war between Japan and China, with its massacres and colossal loss of life; and Jung Chang herself, of course, witnessed the excesses of the Cultural Revolution. *Wild Swans* provides an unflinching record of what the Chinese people have had to endure over the last hundred years but it is far from being a depressing or a dispiriting book. Horror and heartbreak fill its pages but readers will also emerge from them with a renewed sense of the strength of the human spirit to persist and prevail in the worst of circumstances.

⮑Read on

Mao: The Unknown Story (with Jon Halliday)
Adeline Yen Mah, *Falling Leaves*; Aiping Mu, *Vermilion Gate*; Xinran, *The Good Women of China*

PAULO COELHO (b. 1947) BRAZIL

THE ALCHEMIST (1988/1993)

In terms of sales alone, Paulo Coelho is South America's most successful novelist ever, his work translated into dozens of languages and selling millions of copies worldwide. Sophisticated critics may find it easy to deride his parable-like stories and the simple language in which he tells them but he clearly reaches out to readers in search of fiction that combines page-turning narrative with a spiritual message. Coelho has published more than twenty books, including the story of a woman who is strangely liberated by her decision to commit suicide (*Veronika Decides to Die*), a version of the biblical story of Elijah (*The Fifth Mountain*) and the tale of a prostitute's sexual odyssey in search of true love (*Eleven Minutes*). However, his best-known work remains *The Alchemist*, first published in Brazil in 1988 and translated into English five years later. Subtitled 'A Fable About Following Your Dreams', this heartening story of Santiago, an Andalusian shepherd boy who dreams of a treasure in far off Egypt and sets off in search of it, has long been an international bestseller. During his travels, Santiago meets with people who assist him, whether consciously or unconsciously, with his quest and eventually he encounters an alchemist in the desert who becomes his guru and opens his eyes to the true values of life, love and suffering. At the end of the journey, Santiago learns that the treasure he has been pursuing is not at all what he first imagined but he realises that his pilgrimage has had its own intrinsic value, irrespective of what was to be found at its end. During his travels he has become reconciled to his own self and learned to recognise his own purpose in life. As

Coelho writes, 'The boy and his heart had become friends and neither was capable now of betraying the other.'

📖Read on
The Gift; *By the River Piedra I Sat Down and Wept*; *The Zahir*
Mitch Albom, *Tuesdays with Morrie*; Deborah Morrison, *Nexus*

CHARLES DARWIN (1809–82) UK

THE ORIGIN OF SPECIES (1859)

Described by the geneticist Steve Jones as 'the only bestseller to change man's conception of himself', *On the Origin of Species by Means of Natural Selection, or the Preservation of Favoured Races in the Struggle for Life* (to give it the full title it had on first publication) is perhaps unique among undoubtedly paradigm-breaking scientific works in that it can be read with pleasure by a non-scientist. Darwin's subject-matter and his own lucid prose mean that the best way for a general reader to understand the argument Darwin was presenting is to read the original book. In *The Origin of Species*, Darwin argues that species are not, as was assumed at the time, fixed. They evolve over long periods of time. This evolution takes place because, in the struggle to survive and propagate, those organisms best adapted to their environments will ultimately succeed and those less well adapted will die out. As the environment changes, so species will change by a process of 'natural selection'. The naturally occurring variations on which this selection depends are random and not the result of any divine plan, as religious thinkers might argue. The view of nature and man's place in it that the theory of evolution implies is not necessarily a comforting one. Many people, both at the time that Darwin first made his theory public and in the century and a half since, have found it impossible to accept. Yet it is not a petty or a reductionist vision of the universe that unfolds if basic evolutionary ideas are assumed. As Darwin himself wrote at the conclusion of his great work, 'There is grandeur in this view of life, with its several powers, having been originally breathed into a few forms or into one; and that, whilst this planet has gone cycling on according to the fixed law of gravity, from so simple a beginning endless forms most beautiful and most wonderful have been, and are being, evolved.'

🕮Read on

The Descent of Man; *The Voyage of the Beagle*
Richard Dawkins, *The Blind Watchmaker*; Steve Jones, *Almost Like a Whale*

RICHARD DAWKINS (b. 1941) KENYA/UK

THE GOD DELUSION (2006)

Richard Dawkins was born in Kenya and moved to England with his family when he was a boy. Much of his life has been spent at Oxford where he has been undergraduate, graduate student, lecturer in zoology and, since 1995, Professor of Public Understanding of Science. In 1976 he published his first book, *The Selfish Gene*, which became a major popular and critical success and, with its title, added a new expression to the English language. Since then, he has published several more books which have explained Darwinian and evolutionary ideas to the general public (*The Blind Watchmaker*, *Climbing Mount Improbable*) but, in recent years, he has become most famous as the scourge of theologians and religious believers everywhere. When Napoleon asked the mathematician Pierre-Simon Laplace why there was no mention of God in his latest book, the French savant loftily replied, 'Sire, I had no need of that hypothesis.' Like Laplace, Dawkins has no need of that hypothesis. Indeed that hypothesis seems to outrage him and *The God Delusion* is directed against those who still cling to it. It is a no-holds-barred assault on religious belief that pours scorn on the idea that there is a divine designer of the universe and lambasts the often pernicious influence of religion on modern society. Instead it champions the elegant simplicity of Darwin's theory of evolution which Dawkins firmly believes to be sufficient explanation for the diversity of life. His book, unsurprisingly, has not been universally popular despite its bestseller status. He has been accused of indulging in an atheist variety of the very fundamentalism he condemns in others. Yet *The God Delusion*, written with the same wit and cleverness that characterises all of Dawkins's other books, is one of the most powerful polemics published in recent years. After reading it, the traditional idea of an all-knowing and all-seeing God may seem as sensible as belief in Father Christmas.

⮂Read on

The Blind Watchmaker; *Unweaving the Rainbow*
Sam Harris, *The End of Faith*; Christopher Hitchens, *God Is Not Great*

SIMONE DE BEAUVOIR (1908–86) FRANCE

THE SECOND SEX (1949/1953)

Simone de Beauvoir is remembered for her central role in the French philosophical movement known as existentialism and for her lifelong association with Jean-Paul Sartre which began when she was a student at the Sorbonne in Paris and he was attending the École Normale Supérieure in the same city. In their lifetimes it was Sartre who had the greater fame but, two decades after de Beauvoir's death, it could well be argued that it is her reputation and her influence that have lasted the best. Her works range from semi-autobiographical novels (*The Mandarins*, for example) and volumes of memoirs to philosophical essays and political tracts. However, the book which has done most to ensure her place in the history of 20th century thought is undoubtedly *The Second Sex*, a long analysis of the position of women in history and society which was written in the years immediately following the Second World War. Famous for its assertion that, 'One is not born, but rather becomes, a woman', *The Second Sex* is one of the founding texts of modern feminism. De Beauvoir's fundamental argument in the book is that, throughout history, societies have seen humanity in male terms. As she wrote, 'Man is defined as a human being and a woman as a female – whenever she behaves as a human being she is said to imitate the male.' In other words, the human 'norm' is male and the female is somehow the 'other'. In making her case, de Beauvoir draws on a wide range of disciplines from anthropology and sociology to philosophy and history, demonstrating both a prodigious erudition and a skill in posing the most awkward questions about gender and sexuality in the most powerful and direct way. Nearly six decades after it first appeared in French, *The Second Sex* remains one of the classic manifestos of twentieth-century feminism.

≋Read on

The Mandarins (fiction); *Memoirs of a Dutiful Daughter*; *The Prime of Life*; *Force of Circumstance*; *All Said and Done* (four volumes of memoirs)
Judith Butler, *Gender Trouble*; Betty Friedan, *The Feminine Mystique*

JARED DIAMOND (b. 1937) USA

GUNS, GERMS AND STEEL (1997)

A polymath in an age of specialisation, Jared Diamond has made major contributions to knowledge in subjects as diverse as ornithology and human evolution and written bestselling books for the general reader which range widely across disciplines in order to construct thought-provoking theses about the history of man and the history of civilisations. In *The Rise and Fall of the Third Chimpanzee*, he looked at human history in the light of our animal biology and its continuing influence. In *Guns, Germs and Steel*, he asked a very basic historical question. Why is it that for the last 500 years the civilisations of the west have been in the ascendant and have shaped the world in which we live? Or, as a New Guinea friend of Diamond once asked, 'Why is it that you white people developed so much cargo and brought it to New

Guinea but we black people had little cargo of our own?' In the past, arguments have been put forward that depended on assumptions of racial superiority. In his ambitious book, Diamond combines history and science to advance a less pernicious explanation. Going back thousands of years into prehistory, he traces the biogeographical reasons behind the rise of agriculture and the domestication of animals, and the consequences these had for the development of settled societies and more complex civilisations. He explains why Europe and Eurasia were, by chance, the most suitable areas for the encouragement of these trends and places our modern history in a much broader context. 'History followed different courses for different peoples,' he writes, 'because of differences among peoples' environments, not because of biological differences among peoples themselves.' In *Guns, Germs and Steel*, Diamond ranges boldly and confidently through a number of intellectual disciplines in order to produce an immensely thought-provoking book, one which can make readers look at the whole of human history in a different way.

❧Read on

Collapse: How Societies Choose to Fail or Succeed; *The Rise and Fall of the Third Chimpanzee*
John Darwin, *After Tamerlane: The Rise and Fall of Global Empires*; Felipe Fernandez-Armesto, *Civilizations*

PHILIP K. DICK (1928–82) USA

THE MAN IN THE HIGH CASTLE (1962)

A recurring theme in popular culture recently (and indeed in the more esoteric realms of academic philosophy) is the notion that 'reality' is nothing more than a construct and that behind it lurk other, possibly darker truths about the nature of the world in which we live. However, before there was *The Truman Show* and *The Matrix*, before people began to speculate that we might be living in a computer-generated reality, there was Philip K. Dick. Dick, whose work is usually categorised (and sometimes dismissed) as science fiction, wrote books which can still disconcert, disorient and delight readers decades after first publication. Of these, one of the most remarkable is *The Man in the High Castle*. The rewriting of history is a standard idea in science fiction and, at first glance, *The Man in the High Castle* seems a standard example of the subgenre. The Axis powers have won the Second World War and the Japanese and the Germans rule the USA between them. Yet Dick's book soon reveals itself as far more complicated and subtle than a straightforward work of alternative history. It is an interlocking, intermeshing web of possible realities. One of the central characters has written a bestseller in which the Allies won the war and the world looks more like the one we know. An alternate history lies within an alternate history. Who can be sure what the 'true' reality is? Dick plays increasingly complicated games with the idea of 'history' and how accepted versions of it come to be created. When he published *The Man in the High Castle*, Dick had already written other novels (*Time Out of Joint*, for example) which investigated the nature of reality and he went on to produce many other works with a similar theme but this 1962 narrative of alternative history remains his masterpiece.

See also: *100 Must-Read Science Fiction Novels*

≋**Read on**

Do Androids Dream of Electric Sheep?; *Time Out of Joint*; *Valis* Alfred Bester, *The Demolished Man*; Philip Roth, *The Plot Against America*; Norman Spinrad, *The Iron Dream*

FREDERICK DOUGLASS (1818–95) USA

NARRATIVE OF THE LIFE OF FREDERICK DOUGLASS, AN AMERICAN SLAVE (1845)

In the course of an extraordinary life, Frederick Douglass travelled from slavery to a position as one of the most eminent and eloquent campaigners for black freedom and human rights in the nineteenth century. He was born in Maryland, the son of Harriet Bailey, who was a slave, and (in all likelihood) a white father. He was separated from his mother at a very early age and was looked after by his grandmother on a plantation until, still a small child, he was despatched to a new owner in Baltimore. It was his new owner's wife who, contrary to state law, taught him to read and write and thus unwittingly provided him with the means to change his life. In 1838, while working in a shipyard in Baltimore, he fled the city and made his way to New York where he took the name of Douglass, married and (some years later) met the abolitionist and anti-slavery campaigner William Lloyd Garrison. It was Garrison who inspired Douglass to speak at abolitionist meetings and to write the book that was published in 1845 as *Narrative of the Life of Frederick Douglass, an American Slave* and immediately became a bestseller. Douglass went on to write two further volumes of auto-biography and to edit his own abolitionist newspaper, *The North Star*. For the rest of his life, he remained one of the most powerful and compelling advocates of the rights of his fellow African-Americans. His autobiographies reflect the man he was. In a speech delivered towards the end of his life, he said that, 'No man can put a chain about the ankle of his fellow man without at last finding the other end fastened about his own neck.' In his knowledge that slavery diminishes both slave and owner and in his profound belief in the importance of freedom for all men, Frederick Douglass remains an inspiration more than a century after his death.

≷Read on

My Bondage and My Freedom; *Life and Times of Frederick Douglass* (the two later versions of his life that Douglass wrote, publishing them in 1855 and 1881 respectively)

W.E. Du Bois, *The Souls of Black Folk*; Harriet Beecher Stowe, *Uncle Tom's Cabin*

READONATHEME: UP FROM SLAVERY

Olaudah Equiano, *The Interesting Narrative of the Life of Olaudah Equiano*

Harriet Jacobs, *Incidents in the Life of a Slave Girl*

Elizabeth Keckley, *Behind the Scenes, or Thirty Years a Slave and Four Years in the White House*

Mary Prince, *The History of Mary Prince*

Sojourner Truth, *The Narrative of Sojourner Truth*

Booker T. Washington, *Up from Slavery*

Harriet E. Wilson, *Our Nig*

Norman R. Yetman (ed), *When I Was a Slave; Memoirs from the Slave Narrative Collection*

SEBASTIAN FAULKS (b. 1953) UK

BIRDSONG (1993)

In 1910 a young Englishman named Stephen Wraysford arrives in Amiens to stay with the Azaire family. Soon he is embarked on a convention-defying affair with Madame Azaire and, when it is discovered, the two leave Amiens together. The affair does not last and Stephen is left a cold and empty man by its failure, uncaring of what the future might hold for him. What it holds are the trenches of the Great

War. He becomes an officer and takes part in Ypres, the Somme and other major battles of the war, watching men die horribly all around him and discovering in himself a surprisingly steely determination to survive. As the northern France he knew before the war becomes both a quagmire and a slaughterhouse, his past relationship with Madame Azaire resurfaces in an unexpected and disturbing way. Sebastian Faulks has written a number of very good novels in his career. *Charlotte Gray*, set in the Second World War, tells the story of a young woman journeying into France in search of her lover, and *Human Traces* is a massively ambitious saga which follows the fortunes of two pioneering psychiatrists. None, however, has matched the power of *Birdsong* nor enjoyed its commercial and critical success. It is not difficult to work out the reasons why this novel of love and war has proved such a triumph for him. The power of his writing, both in its evocation of the passionate affair and in its descriptions of the claustrophobia and terror of the trenches, is remarkable. He succeeds both in conveying the comradeship of men in battle and in precisely observing the ebb and flow of an intense romantic relationship. Few modern novels capture readers' imaginations so fully as *Birdsong* does. It shows individuals trapped by historical events over which they have no control and poignantly records their efforts to retain their humanity in inhumane circumstances.

⮒Read on

Charlotte Gray; *Human Traces*
Pat Barker, *Regeneration* (and its successors *The Eye in the Door* and *The Ghost Road*); Louis de Bernières, *Captain Corelli's Mandolin*; Erich Maria Remarque, *All Quiet on the Western Front*

ANNE FRANK (1929–45) THE NETHERLANDS

THE DIARY OF ANNE FRANK (1947/1952)

The heart-rending story of how a young Jewish girl from Amsterdam hid with her family from the Nazis until they were found and sent to a concentration camp became an instant classic when it was first published in English in 1952. More than half a century later the story of a teenager coming to maturity in the most terrible of circumstances remains profoundly moving. Anne Frank was actually born in Germany but her family moved to Holland when she was a small child. She was 11 years old when the Germans occupied the Netherlands and 13 when the Franks, together with four fellow Jews, went into hiding in a small set of rooms above the premises used by her father's business. They stayed there for just over two years until someone betrayed their hiding place to the Nazis. The Franks were arrested and transported first to the small concentration camp of Westerbork and then to Auschwitz. Anne and her sister Margot were transferred to Belsen where they both died in a typhus epidemic in March of 1945, only weeks before the camp was liberated by Allied troops. Her father, Otto Frank, survived his time in Auschwitz and, after the war, it was he who retrieved his daughter's diary, written during her 24 months in hiding, and arranged its publication. Anne Frank became perhaps the best-known of all victims of the Holocaust and her words continue to be read decades after her death. 'It's difficult in times like these: ideals, dreams and cherished hopes rise within us, only to be crushed by grim reality,' she wrote. 'It's a wonder I haven't abandoned all my ideals, they seem so absurd and impractical. Yet I cling to them because I still believe, in spite of everything, that people are truly good at heart.'

⊗Read on

Tales from the Secret Annexe

Mary Berg, *The Diary of Mary Berg*; Livia Bitton-Jackson, *I Have Lived a Thousand Years*; Janusz Korczak, *Ghetto Diary*

VICTOR FRANKL (1905–97) AUSTRIA

MAN'S SEARCH FOR MEANING (1946/1959)

Victor Frankl was born into a prominent Jewish family in Vienna and, after studying medicine at university, he specialised in psychiatry, showing a particular interest in the still controversial ideas of psychoanalysts like Freud and Adler. Before the *Anschluss* of 1938, the Nazi annexation of Austria, Frankl had already won a reputation as a pioneering specialist in the treatment of suicidal patients but, under the anti-semitic legislation of the Nazis, he found it increasingly difficult to work. Eventually, in 1942, he was arrested and, together with most of the members of his close family, he was despatched to a concentration camp. Frankl survived the war; most of his family, including his wife and his parents, did not. His 1946 book, translated as *Man's Search for Meaning*, chronicled his experiences in the war and is the founding text of his school of psychotherapy, usually known as 'logotherapy'. The book's original German title ('*... trotzdem ja zum Leben sagen*') can be literally translated as 'Saying Yes to Life Regardless' and that provides as precise a summary of Frankl's ideas as it is possible to get. At the heart of logotherapy is the idea that life has meaning even in the midst of terrible suffering and that the urge to find that meaning and assert it provides the most fundamental motivation for living. Frankl's experiences in the Holocaust both tested his theories in the most extreme of circumstances and enabled him to refine and develop them. As he wrote, 'We have come to know man as he really is.' 'Man,' he went on to say, 'is that being who invented the gas chambers of Auschwitz; however, he is also that being who entered those gas chambers upright, with the Lord's Prayer or the *Shema Yisrael* on his lips.'

⮂Read on

Man's Search for Ultimate Meaning
Rollo May, *Love and Will*; Carl Rogers, *On Becoming a Person*

SIGMUND FREUD (1856–1939) AUSTRIA

THE INTERPRETATION OF DREAMS (1900/1913)

Sigmund Freud was born in the small Moravian town of Freiburg and his family moved to Vienna when he was four years old. He lived there until he was an old man of eighty-two, through all the years in which he slowly elaborated his theories about sexuality, the unconscious mind and the hidden motives behind human action. Only when the Nazis marched into Vienna in 1938 and Freud, as both a Jew and a supposedly 'decadent' thinker, found his life was in danger, did he move from the city, going into exile in London where he died in the following year. Freud's contribution to modern thought is almost incalculable. His influence permeates our culture to such an extent that it is perfectly possible to be aware of Freudian ideas without ever having read a book by him. Which of his many published works, however, is the most significant? Freud himself was certain enough. Dreams were the gateways to the unconscious mind or, as he put it, 'The interpretation of dreams is the royal road to a knowledge of the unconscious activities of the mind.' And his book *The Interpretation of Dreams* included some of his profoundest thinking. 'Insights such as this,' he wrote, 'fall to one's lot but once in a lifetime.' In his monumental work on dreams, he provides a route map of the royal roads to the unconscious. He reveals how we disguise our true motivations and desires, the 'latent' content of the dream, behind its 'manifest' content (what we remember of it) and how we can access our hidden selves. Dreams, with all their mysteries and ambiguities, have always haunted us. Thanks to Freud we have new ways of understanding them and of using them to learn more about our secret thoughts and longings. After Freud, we can never quite see ourselves as we once did.

≋Read on

Civilization and Its Discontents; *Three Essays on the Theory of Sexuality*
C.G. Jung, *Dreams*

ERICH FROMM (1900–80) GERMANY/USA

THE ART OF LOVING (1956)

Born in Frankfurt and educated there and at Heidelberg University, Fromm trained as a psychoanalyst in the 1920s and was already a respected practitioner in Germany when the Nazis came to power in 1933. As a Jew, he was under an immediate threat both personally and professionally and he moved first to Switzerland and then to the USA. He spent the rest of his working life as an academic in American universities. Fromm was a prolific writer and his works range from *The Fear of Freedom* and *The Sane Society*, which examine the structures of modern society from a psychological perspective, to books on Marx, Freud and the links between psychoanalysis and Zen Buddhism. However, his most lasting legacy may well prove to be a short book he wrote in the 1950s in which he explored the nature of love and its capacity to alter lives for the better. *The Art of Loving* is not the kind of simplistic self-help book that the title might immediately suggest. Rather it is a clear-sighted exploration of what love (from brotherly love, the love of one's fellows which Fromm believed formed the basis for all other love, to erotic love) might be. In Fromm's eyes, modern society and modern capitalism work to undermine the many different varieties of love and encourage the kind of selfishness and alienation from others that is love's very antithesis. Only through hard work and self-examination can people achieve the capacity for genuine and fulfilling love. Fromm argues that, although it provides no magic answers to life's difficulties and although our expectations of it are often unrealistic, then none the less 'Love is the only sane and satisfactory answer to the problem of human existence.' For more than fifty years readers of *The Art of Loving* have found truth in his assertion.

⭲Read on
The Fear of Freedom; *The Sane Society*; *To Have or To Be*
John Armstrong, *Conditions of Love*; Thomas Lewis, *A General Theory of Love*

JOSTEIN GAARDER (b. 1952) NORWAY

SOPHIE'S WORLD (1991/1995)
Jostein Gaarder is a onetime philosophy teacher who has become one of Scandinavia's most popular writers for both children and adults. His best-known work, first published in Norway in 1991 and in the UK four years later, is *Sophie's World*. This focuses on a fourteen-year-old Norwegian girl named Sophie Amundsen whose life is turned upside down when she finds notes in her mailbox posing two questions: Who are you? Where does the world come from? In attempting to find answers to them, she becomes involved with an enigmatic middle-aged gentleman called Alberto Knox who takes her on a whistlestop tour of world philosophy from Plato to modern physics. In many ways, *Sophie's World* is an unlikely candidate for bestseller status. The plot of the novel sometimes seems a perfunctory excuse for introducing Alberto's philosophy lessons. The book really is as much a guide to western philosophy as it is a compelling story. And yet something in

Gaarder's narrative spoke very directly to its millions of readers. Probably the secret of its success lies in its ability to strip away the unnecessary complexities and over-elaborations that so often attach themselves to the subject of philosophy and to reveal the fundamentals beneath. Philosophy is not (or should not be) primarily about ideas that are only accessible to academics or intellectuals. It asks the basic questions that occur to any human being who has ever thought about the world and his or her place in it. And it attempts to find open-ended answers that will help us all to make sense of our experiences. At one point in the novel, Sophie is told that, 'The only thing we require to be good philosophers is the faculty of wonder'. Jostein Gaarder's great achievement is that his story succeeds in stimulating and encouraging that faculty.

≋Read on

Maya; *The Solitaire Mystery*

Alain de Botton, *How Proust Can Change Your Life*; Catherine Clement, *Theo's Odyssey*

MOHANDAS K. GANDHI (1869–1948) INDIA

THE STORY OF MY EXPERIMENTS WITH TRUTH
(1927–29)

Today Gandhi is remembered as the charismatic Indian leader whose method of non-violent resistance to oppression (*satyagraha*) played a major role in forcing the British Raj to grant independence to his country. It was an independence that the Mahatma was not able to experience for long – he was assassinated in January 1948 by a Hindu extremist outraged by his willingness to tolerate non-Hindus in the new India – but he continues to be a revered figure throughout the nation that he did so much to create. However, his autobiography, originally entitled *The Story of My Experiments with Truth*, was first written and published some time before he achieved the iconic, indeed almost saintly status he was granted during his last years. The book is not a conventional autobiography. Indeed some readers might argue that it is not an autobiography at all. It draws upon his experiences in life but its focus, as its title suggests, is upon his search for truth. To Gandhi the only path to truth was one which turned its back on egotism. 'The seeker after truth should be humbler than dust,' he wrote. 'The world crushes the dust under its feet, but the seeker after truth should so humble himself that even the dust could crush him. Only then, and not till then, will he have a glimpse of truth.' Through the simple living, the self-purification and the spiritual commitment which he chronicles in his book, Gandhi hoped to gain a glimpse of the truth himself. The British politician Sir Stafford Cripps, paying tribute to him after his assassination, said that he knew of no other man 'who so convincingly demonstrated the power of the spirit over material things'. That power is quietly and undemonstratively revealed in Gandhi's 'autobiography'.

Read on

Louis Fischer, *The Life of Mahatma Gandhi*; John Ruskin, *Unto This Last*; Rabindranath Tagore, *Gitanjali*

KAHLIL GIBRAN (1883–1931) LEBANON/USA

THE PROPHET (1923)

Born into a Christian Maronite community in the Lebanon, then part of the Ottoman Empire, Kahlil Gibran travelled with his mother and his siblings to America in 1895 in search of a better life. He was to return to Lebanon in the years to come and spent time in Europe but essentially America became his home. In the early years of the twentieth century, Gibran suffered devastating loss, with the deaths of his mother and two of his siblings, but he also came to the attention of an older woman who was to be his patron for the rest of his life. Mary Haskell, a respected teacher and educator in Boston, encouraged his creative work. Before 1918, this work consisted largely of paintings and poetry in Arabic but, determined to reach as wide an audience as possible, he began later to write in English. Books such as *The Madman* (1918) and *The Forerunner* (1920) followed but Gibran's biggest success by far came with *The Prophet*, a volume which has become one of the bestselling inspirational books of all time. These poetic essays on the meaning of life record the wisdom of a mysterious prophet, about to embark on a journey, who has nothing to offer the people gathered to witness his departure but the answers to the questions each of them puts to him. In the rich and resonant language his creator gives him, the prophet reveals his thoughts on everything in life from love and marriage to the enigmas of birth and death. In one of the sections of *The Prophet*, Gibran wrote that, 'You give but little when you give of your possessions./It is when you give of yourself that you truly give.' Through his writings, his own gift of himself continues to be appreciated by readers decades after his untimely death.

≋Read on

The Madman; *The Forerunner*

Dag Hammarskjold, *Markings*; Anne Morrow Lindbergh, *Gift from the Sea*; Rumi, *Selected Poems*; Rabindranath Tagore, *Gitanjali*

JEAN GIONO (1895–1970) FRANCE

THE MAN WHO PLANTED TREES (1954)

In a literary career that lasted for more than forty years, Jean Giono won much acclaim. Particularly in his native France, his historical fiction (*The Horseman on the Roof*) and his powerful, unsentimental novels set in the Provençal countryside which he loved (*Second Harvest, Song of the World*) are considered twentieth-century classics. Yet it could easily be argued that his most remarkable and long-lasting achievement is a short parable, published in France in 1953, which first appeared in an English translation in the magazine *Vogue* the following year. *The Man Who Planted Trees* consists of less than 5,000 words but it is a story that, once read, remains in the mind and imagination. It opens in 1910 when the unnamed narrator is hiking through some of the wilder regions of Provence. In a remote and treeless valley he comes across a shepherd named Elzéard Bouffier. Bouffier has undertaken the self-imposed task of revivifying the barren land. He is planting thousands and thousands of trees. Over the decades, the narrator returns occasionally to Bouffier's valley and is witness to its startling transformation. When Bouffier dies, nearly four decades after his first meeting with the narrator, the once desolate valley is a green and pleasant Eden. Translated into many languages, *The Man Who Planted Trees* has become by far Giono's most widely read and most loved work. In the final analysis it succeeds so well with readers all around the world because its message is an optimistic and uplifting one. One man, it says, can make a difference. As the narrator remarks, 'When I reflect that one man, armed only with his own physical and moral resources, was able to cause this land of Canaan to spring from the wasteland, I am convinced that in spite of everything, humanity is admirable.'

🔖 Read on
Second Harvest
Roger Deakin, *Wildwood: A Journey Through Trees*; Marcel Pagnol, *Jean de Florette*

MALCOLM GLADWELL (b. 1963) UK/CANADA

THE TIPPING POINT (2000)

Some books change us as individuals; others change the way in which we look at the world. Of books in the latter category published in the last decade, one of the most eye-opening has been Malcolm Gladwell's *The Tipping Point*. After reading it, a whole host of social phenomena seem more readily explicable than they did before. Gladwell argues that the best way of understanding many of the things that happen in contemporary society – from the dramatic success of Harry Potter to change in the patterns of violent crime – is to think of them as behaving like epidemics. Certain ideas and products and behaviours spread like a virus. They pass from person to person and, like epidemics, they can gather momentum very rapidly and then suddenly surge through society. They have a 'tipping point', a point at which they reach critical mass and become almost unstoppable. His central idea owes much to Richard Dawkins's theory of the 'meme', first formulated in *The Selfish Gene*, but Gladwell takes it and gives it new and unexpected applications. He provides his readers with a new and surprisingly powerful tool for decoding the world around them and making sense of it. The idea of social behaviour as an epidemic may seem disconcerting or even distressing but, as Gladwell is eager to point out, it is ultimately an optimistic one. His book is about change and how change happens. And one of its central arguments is that large-scale change can often be the result of changes at a microcosmic level. However powerless the individual might seem to be, he or she can make a difference in the world Gladwell describes. 'What must underlie successful epidemics, in the end,' he writes, 'is a bedrock belief that change is possible, that people can radically transform their behaviour or beliefs in the face of the right kind of impetus.'

⮥Read on

Blink

Susan Blackmore, *The Meme Machine*; Richard Dawkins, *The Selfish Gene*; Steven D. Levitt & Stephen J. Dubner, *Freakonomics*

DANIEL GOLEMAN (b. 1946) USA

EMOTIONAL INTELLIGENCE (1995)

The son of two academics, Goleman grew up in California and went on to receive a doctorate in psychology from Harvard. For many years he was a science journalist, writing on the brain and behavioural sciences for the *New York Times* and publishing a well-received book on the psychology of meditation. In 1995, he produced a worldwide bestseller in *Emotional Intelligence*, a book that, with its argument that good emotional skills are more important in creating a successful life than traditional notions of IQ, struck a chord with millions of readers.

Goleman highlighted the dangers both of unthinking indulgence in emotions and of alienation from one's own feelings and those of others. 'If your emotional abilities aren't in hand,' he wrote, 'if you don't have self-awareness, if you are not able to manage your distressing emotions, if you can't have empathy and have effective relationships, then no matter how smart you are, you are not going to get very far.' In many ways, the concept of 'Emotional Intelligence' emerges from the observation of everyday life (surely we all know of individuals who either act disastrously on impulse or who have intellectual capacities which outrun their abilities to interact with others) but Goleman's book provides scientific backing for commonsense. And it also provides the kind of advice on ways to improve our lives that the best self-help books do. The structure of our brains may not have changed much over millennia and, in many ways, our feelings may well be better designed for life in the prehistoric era rather than the post-modern world but we need not despair. We can unlearn some emotions and we can encourage others and, by doing so, we can gain a control over our lives that we did not previously have. There is a practical optimism in *Emotional Intelligence* which goes a long way towards explaining its success.

⮂Read on

Social Intelligence; *Working with Emotional Intelligence*
Stephen R. Covey, *The Seven Habits of Highly Effective People*;
Thomas Harris, *I'm OK, You're OK*

GERMAINE GREER (b. 1939) AUSTRALIA/UK

THE FEMALE EUNUCH (1970)

Germaine Greer, educated at the Universities of Melbourne, Sydney and Cambridge, was working as a lecturer in English literature and as a journalist for the underground press when the publication of *The Female Eunuch* turned her into one of the intellectual stars of the so-called 'second wave' of feminism. Much of the attention the book attracted was the result of its uncompromising statements about male misogyny ('Women have very little idea how much men hate them', for example) but, at its heart is the wish that women would embrace the chance for true freedom that the times seemed to offer them. 'The fear of freedom is strong in us,' Greer wrote. 'We call it chaos or anarchy, and the words are threatening.' Her book is a demand that women should ignore the fear and plunge into the scarily exciting world that freedom from conventional ideas about femininity and the relationships between the sexes opened up. Since the publication of *The Female Eunuch*, Germaine Greer has enjoyed a long and often controversial career. She has written on a vast range of subjects from female painters and the barriers placed in their path throughout the centuries (*The Obstacle Race*) to women's experiences of the menopause (*The Change*), her own early life in Australia (*Daddy, We Hardly Knew You*) and the relationship between Shakespeare and Anne Hathaway (*Shakespeare's Wife*). Whatever the subject on which she chooses to write, she brings her own highly distinctive intelligence and sensibility to bear upon it but, nearly four decades after it was first published, *The Female Eunuch* remains her most challenging book. The wittiest of all

47

feminist polemics, it continues to be a liberating read for women (and men), charting the ways in which traditional, patriarchal ideas about the relations between the sexes oppress us all.

⪮Read on

The Whole Woman ('This sequel to *The Female Eunuch* is the book I said I would never write,' as Greer wrote)

Shulamith Firestone, *The Dialectic of Sex*; Gloria Steinem, *Outrageous Acts and Everyday Rebellions*

READONATHEME: WOMANPOWER

Betty Friedan, *The Second Stage*

Bell Hooks, *Ain't I a Woman?*

Kate Millett, *Sexual Politics*

Adrienne Rich, *Of Woman Born*

Sheila Rowbotham, *Woman's Consciousness, Man's World*

Dale Spender, *Women of Ideas (And What Men Have Done to Them)*

Mary Wollstonecraft, *A Vindication of the Rights of Woman*

G.I. GURDJIEFF (1872?–1949) ARMENIA

MEETINGS WITH REMARKABLE MEN (1963)

Much about Gurdjieff's early life is mysterious (even the exact date of his birth is unknown) but he is said to have spent long periods of it travelling in the Middle East, India and Central Asia, learning about various spiritual traditions. He began his career as teacher and guru in Tsarist Russia but was forced into flight and eventual exile by the upheaval of the Bolshevik Revolution in 1917. By the mid-1920s, he had settled in Paris where he spent most of the rest of his life and where he created establishments such as the 'Institute for the Harmonious Development of Man' to propagate his ideas. At the heart of his philosophy is the notion that most people are not fully awake to the realities of existence and that they sleepwalk their way through life. 'Man lives his life in sleep, and in sleep he dies', he is quoted as saying in a book by his leading disciple, P.D. Ouspensky. The work of self-development which Gurdjieff proposed involved techniques that would promote awareness of the self and of the world and would awaken the individual to a fuller experience of reality. *Meetings with Remarkable Men*, first published after Gurdjieff's death, is a strange hybrid of a book, an eclectic mix of travel literature, memoir and spiritual advice that reflects the unusual personality of its author. To some, it reveals that he was essentially a charlatan; to others, it is the best introduction to a man who was one of the great spiritual teachers of the twentieth century. 'Knowledge and understanding are quite different,' Gurdjieff wrote in its pages. 'Only understanding can lead to being, whereas knowledge is but a passing presence in it.' For those who admire his work, Gurdjieff's writings provide a direct path to that kind of understanding.

⊜Read on

Beelzebub's Tales to His Grandson; *Life is Real Only Then, When I Am*
P.D. Ouspensky, *The Fourth Way*

ALEX HALEY (1921–92) USA

ROOTS (1976)

In 1976, Alex Haley, a former officer in the US Coast Guard and star interviewer for *Playboy*, published a book which claimed to trace back his family to an eighteenth-century African named Kunta Kinte who had been captured by slavers and brought to America to work in the plantations. The book was *Roots* and it became a bestseller. The TV mini-series based on it was equally successful. In the thirty years since its first publication, *Roots* has had plenty of critics. Doubts have been expressed about the validity of Haley's research and his success in identifying his genuine slave ancestor, the village in Africa from which he came and the ship on which he was taken to America has been questioned. Many would say that the book is largely a work of the imagination rather than historical scholarship. Nonetheless it is difficult to deny the significance of Haley's work. For millions and millions of African-Americans, *Roots* provided a new pride in their ancestry and a new awareness of the rich cultural heritage that was theirs. Yet the book does not only speak to black Americans. As Haley wrote, 'In all of us there is a hunger, marrow deep, to know our heritage – to know who we are and where we came from.' For all of us, without this, 'there is a hollow yearning. No matter what our attainments in life, there is still a vacuum, an emptiness, and the most disquieting loneliness.' For this reason, *Roots* speaks to people of all races and from all nations. And, in its story of a young man transported across an ocean and his descendants' struggle against the brutal realities of slavery, it provides eloquent testimony to the ability of the human spirit to survive in the worst of circumstances.

⮒Read on

Queen (Haley traces the other side of his family back to the illegitimate daughter of a white plantation owner in a book left unfinished at his death and completed by his friend David Stevens)
Melton McLaurin, *Celia, a Slave: A True Story*; Hugh Thomas, *The Slave Trade*

STEPHEN HAWKING (b. 1942) UK

A BRIEF HISTORY OF TIME (1988)

Stephen Hawking is probably the most famous scientist in the world today. Like Einstein before him, he has become a representative figure in the public mind of the kind of people who undertake the most vaulting speculations about the universe. That he has become so is probably a consequence of two things. One is the runaway success of his book *A Brief History of Time* which has sold millions of copies worldwide since its first publication. The second is the fact that Hawking suffers from the terrible long-term effects of motor neurone disease. That the mind which makes such enormous leaps and bounds of the imagination is trapped within a wasted and wheelchair-confined body has an ironic poignancy that fixes Hawking in the public imagination. Since 1979 he has been Lucasian Professor of Mathematics at Cambridge (a position once held by Sir Isaac Newton) and he has long been at the forefront of attempts to combine the two great achievements of modern physics – quantum theory and relativity – into one grand theory. However, it has been *A Brief History of Time* which has brought him the greatest fame and public recognition. Ever since it was first published, jokes have been made about its formidable density and the inability of most people who began it to finish it but the jokes are unfair. *A Brief History of Time* is actually a very elegantly written and lucid survey of man's attempts to understand the universe from the time of the Ancient Greeks to the present day. For non-scientists it represents an opportunity to introduce themselves to the kind of advanced answers that scientists are giving to the profoundest questions about the origin, nature and eventual destiny of the universe. We too can learn about the exhilarating search, in Hawking's metaphor, 'to know the mind of God'.

≋Read on

Black Holes and Baby Universes
Brian Greene, *The Elegant Universe*; Michio Kaku, *Hyperspace*

JOSEPH HELLER (1923–99) USA

CATCH-22 (1961)

The madness of war has never been better captured than in the pages of Heller's novel about US bomber pilots stationed on a Mediterranean island during the Second World War. Damned if they fly their missions and damned if they don't, the men are caught in the vicious circle that is Catch-22. If you're crazy, you won't have to fly. All you need to do is ask. If, however, you ask to be grounded because what you're doing is crazy, that proves you're sane and you have to fly. As Yossarian, the anti-hero of Heller's black comedy, remarks, 'That's some catch, that catch-22'. Around the central figure of Yossarian, a man who measures his sanity against the insanity of the system, swirls a large cast of memorable characters. There is Milo Minderbinder, the lunatic entrepreneur who takes the freedom of the market to such wild extremes that he ends by signing contracts for bombing missions with the Germans and arranging for the dropping of explosives on his own base. There is Major Major Major, a man condemned to ridicule by the convergence of his name and his army rank. There is a battalion of gung-ho top brass who never spare a moment's thought for the poor saps who actually fly the missions. Heller went on to write other novels such as *Something Happened* and *Good as Gold* but none had quite the enormous success that *Catch-22* had. Perhaps that success was a consequence of Heller's first-hand knowledge of the world of which he wrote in his finest novel. As a young man he had served as a bombardier in the US Air Force and had flown from bases in Italy on dozens of missions. In *Catch-22*, he looks at the horrors of war and violence and invites us to laugh in the dark.

⊜**Read on**

Good as Gold; *Closing Time*

Jaroslav Hasek, *The Good Soldier Svejk*; Norman Mailer, *The Naked and the Dead*

EUGEN HERRIGEL (1884–1955) GERMANY

ZEN IN THE ART OF ARCHERY (1948/1953)

Eugen Herrigel, a German academic, lived in Japan in the 1920s and, whilst he was there, he studied *kyudo* or Japanese archery. On his return to Europe, he wrote a short essay on his experiences and he expanded this into a book, first published in German soon after the Second World War. An English version of the book appeared two years before Herrigel's death, with a foreword by the famous Japanese exponent of Zen, D.T. Suzuki. Over the decades since the publication of *Zen in the Art of Archery* it has sometimes been suggested that Herrigel misunderstood both the nature of Zen and the practice of *kyudo* but his book has long become established as a classic account of a Westerner encountering the very different mindset of Eastern thinkers. In his study of *kyudo* the German professor needs to learn that technical expertise and technical knowledge are not enough. What is needed is the ability to go beyond these and reach a stage where the body completes complex and difficult actions without the conscious intervention of the mind. The body achieves control; the conscious self disappears. It is a state of being with which most great sportsmen are probably familiar in some form and it will not be reached if the archer refuses to surrender to it. As Herrigel's teacher tells him, 'The right shot, at the right moment, does not come because you do not let go of yourself.' Through years of training with his teacher, Herrigel not only moves slowly towards skill as an archer but he also nudges his way towards new ways of seeing the world and our interaction with it. 'Fundamentally the marksman aims at himself,' is another of the aphorisms his teacher passes on to him and *Zen and the Art of Archery* records the transformation of that self.

⮁Read on

The Method of Zen

Gustie Herrigel, *Zen in the Art of Flower Arrangement*; D.T. Suzuki, *The Zen Doctrine of No-Mind*; Shunryu Suzuki, *Zen Mind, Beginner's Mind*

HERMANN HESSE (1877–1962) GERMANY

SIDDHARTHA (1922/1951)

Poet, novelist, mystic and winner of the 1946 Nobel Prize for Literature, Hermann Hesse was influenced both by Carl Gustav Jung and, later, by Buddhist philosophy. Hesse's knowledge of Jungian ideas is reflected in many of his novels, including *Demian* and *Steppenwolf*. The importance of Buddhism to his views on life can be seen most clearly in *Siddhartha*, a novel which follows the spiritual journey of its eponymous character, an Indian man living in the sixth century BC, at the same time as the Buddha. At the heart of the novel's story are the varying, often conflicting demands of the contemplative life and the active life. Siddhartha, born into a Brahmin family, is drawn to the extreme asceticism of the wandering holy men known as Samanas who visit his village. Against his father's wishes, he joins the Samanas and seeks enlightenment through the renunciation of the world. Self-denial does not prove the correct path for Siddhartha and nor does his later indulgence in the pleasures of the world. Even encounters with Gotama, the Buddha, provide confusion and fresh questions rather than the answers to life's mysteries which Siddhartha seeks. It is only when he decides to live and work alongside the ferryman Vasudeva, listening to the sounds of the river and contemplating the cycle without beginning and end that connects all life, that Siddhartha finally begins to achieve the enlightenment he has so long and so fruitlessly sought. Eventually Siddhartha comes to believe that, 'Wisdom is not communicable.' As he goes on to say, 'Knowledge can be communicated, but not wisdom. One can find it, live it, be fortified by it, do wonders through it, but one cannot communicate and teach it.' One of the ironies of Hesse's novel is that many of its admirers would argue that it does just that.

See also: *100 Must-Read Books for Men*

📖Read on
Steppenwolf
Thomas Mann, *The Holy Sinner*

S.E. HINTON (b. 1948) USA

THE OUTSIDERS (1967)

Only a handful of novels for teenagers are actually written by teenagers. Most are the work of older writers who are likely to have forgotten what the experience of being a teenager is like. S.E. Hinton's *The Outsiders*, however, was begun when the author was 15 and finally published when she was 18. Hinton knew the world of which she wrote from the inside.

Her book is narrated by Ponyboy Curtis, a sensitive and intelligent fourteen-year-old boy whose parents have recently died in a car crash. He lives with his two older brothers in the impoverished East Side area of a large, unnamed American town. In Ponyboy's world there are two entirely different tribes of people. There are 'greasers' and there are 'socs'. Socs have the money and the social position. Greasers come from the wrong side of the tracks. Ponyboy and his brothers are greasers and are therefore sworn enemies of socs. The novel follows the bitter rivalry between the two gangs, which spirals increasingly into violence, and Ponyboy's relationship with two doomed friends, Dallas and Johnny. It is Johnny who, on his deathbed, urges Ponyboy to 'stay gold', a poignant reference to a Robert Frost poem which Ponyboy has quoted earlier in the novel. Ponyboy eventually vows to forsake the fighting and the tribal warfare between greasers and socs for Johnny's sake and he begins to write the story that, we assume, will become the novel we have just read. *The Outsiders* is often overwrought, melodramatic and sentimental but it has a power to move readers that transcends its faults. They care about Ponyboy and his struggles to understand his traumatic experiences of love and death. Hinton has written more sophisticated novels in her later career but she has never written one that has been as successful or touched as many people so directly.

🕮**Read on**
That Was Then, This Is Now; *Rumble Fish*
Melvyn Burgess, *Junk*

DOUGLAS HOFSTADTER (b. 1945) US

GÖDEL, ESCHER, BACH (1979)

The son of a Nobel Prize-winning physicist, Douglas Hofstadter began his career as a mathematician and physicist himself but he is most famous for *Gödel, Escher, Bach* which has become a classic investigation, unorthodox and digressive, into the workings of the human mind. He takes as his starting points the music of J.S. Bach, the artwork of M.C. Escher and the mathematical theories of Kurt Gödel and he weaves them all into an eye-opening and thought-provoking examination of the power of human creativity and thought and the nature of identity. Playful and paradoxical, the work is full of puns and puzzles, games and stories. Chapters which further the argument alternate with dialogues between imaginary characters that refer back to one another and to the main text. The book remains indefinable and difficult to pin down. When given the opportunity to describe how *he* would define it, Hofstadter said that it was 'a very personal attempt to say how it is that animate beings can come out of inanimate matter. What is a self, and how can a self come out of stuff that is as selfless as a stone or a puddle?' In the years since *Gödel, Escher, Bach*, Hofstadter has published a number of other books. He collaborated with the philosopher and neuroscientist Daniel Dennett to bring together a mind-stretching collection of essays and fictions on identity and consciousness entitled *The Mind's I*, which included contributions by people ranging from Alan Turing to Jorge Luis Borges. *I Am a Strange Loop*, published in 2007, revisited some of the territory of his first book. However, thirty years on, *Gödel, Escher, Bach* remains unique – a wonderful, if demanding, read. Breathtaking in its ambition and its ability to cross boundaries and to jump exhilaratingly from one intellectual discipline to another, it continues to provide an epic adventure for the mind.

⮂Read on

The Mind's I; *I Am a Strange Loop*
Daniel Dennett, *Consciousness Explained*; Gerald Edelman, *Wider than the Sky*

ALDOUS HUXLEY (1894–1963) UK

THE DOORS OF PERCEPTION (1954)

Best remembered today for *Brave New World*, his dystopian vision of a biologically engineered future, Huxley was a polymath from a distinguished intellectual family. In the 1920s and 1930s, he became famous for glittering and mordantly satirical novels about rich and clever people struggling to find meaning in their essentially trivial lives. He moved to the USA in 1937 where he worked as a Hollywood scriptwriter. He lived in America for the rest of his life, continuing to publish a wide range of both fiction and non-fiction. *The Doors of Perception* is an account of his experiments in the 1950s with mind-altering drugs, particularly mescaline. Huxley took his title from the English poet and mystic William Blake. In one of his prophetic books of the 1790s, Blake wrote, 'If the doors of perception were cleansed everything would appear to man as it is, infinite.' Huxley clearly believed that mescaline 'cleansed' his mind. Throughout his descriptions of his experiments, he emphasises that what he was experiencing was not a vision but a heightened version of reality. When he looks again at a vase of flowers he had admired before taking the drug, he sees so much more than he had earlier. 'I was not looking now at an unusual flower arrangement,' Huxley writes. 'I was seeing what Adam had seen on the morning of his creation – the miracle, moment by moment, of naked existence.' When someone asks him whether the experience is agreeable, he replies, 'Neither agreeable nor disagreeable. It just is.' *The Doors of Perception* is a remarkable book. It is an honest and memorable record of what one exceptionally intelligent and sensitive man experienced under the influence of mind-expanding drugs. Reading it can still expand the minds of those who approach the book with the same willingness to 'be shaken out of the ruts of ordinary perception' that inspired its author.

See also: *100 Must-Read Classic Novels*

Read on

Moksha; *The Perennial Philosophy*
Albert Hoffman, *LSD: My Problem Child*; Daniel Pinchbeck, *Breaking Open the Head*

WILLIAM JAMES (1842–1910) USA

THE VARIETIES OF RELIGIOUS EXPERIENCE (1902)

The son of the leading exponent of Swedenborgian ideas in America and the elder brother of the novelist Henry James, William James entered Harvard to study medicine in 1861. He was to spend nearly all the rest of his life attached to the university in some capacity, latterly as professor of philosophy and psychology. In the 1890s, James's interest focused more and more on metaphysical questions of the existence of God, life after death and religious belief. Characteristically, for a philosopher who was a leading exponent of a brand of pragmatism which claimed that abstract ideas are only of value if experience proves that they work in the material world, James approached these questions with the aim of investigating them empirically. He collaborated with psychical researchers to look into the possibility of survival after death and he examined the nature of religious belief by looking at the records of religious experience. The culmination of this work was his most famous book, *The Varieties of Religious Experience*, which had its origin in a series of lectures he gave on the other side of the Atlantic to Harvard, at the University of Edinburgh. James's focus in the book is on the individual's experience of religion rather than the rituals and beliefs of any particular faith or church. After analysis of personal accounts, he concludes that the validity of religious belief resides in the emotional fulfilment that it offers the individual believer rather than in its objective 'truth'. The particulars of faith are 'true' insofar as they supply the emotional needs. More than a century after its first publication, James's *magnum opus* retains its validity and its ability to throw light on why and how human beings express their sense of the numinous and the spiritual.

≋Read on

The Will to Believe
Mircea Eliade, *The Sacred and the Profane*; Rudolf Otto, *The Idea of the Holy*

C.G. JUNG (1875–1961) SWITZERLAND

MEMORIES, DREAMS, REFLECTIONS (1962)

The son of a Lutheran pastor, Jung was born in Switzerland and studied medicine at the University of Basel. Choosing to specialise in psychiatry, he went on to work at the Burghölzli mental hospital in Zurich and it was while he was there that he first became aware of the ideas of Freud, then little known outside Vienna. Jung was enthralled by them and, for a number of years, he was Freud's most ardent and, after the two men had met, most favoured disciple. Jung, however, was not the kind of man likely to remain a disciple for life and he and Freud came to a parting of the ways in 1912. The split was traumatic for both men but especially for Jung who came close to complete breakdown. He emerged from his long dark night of the soul with the path clear before him to move towards the wide-ranging ideas of his own mature theories of human personality, usually known as 'analytic psychology'. The rest of his long life was spent in working out the meanings and implications of these ideas. It is to Jung that we owe the concepts of 'extrovert' and 'introvert' personalities, of psychological archetypes and of the collective unconscious. He affected the way in which we think about the human mind more profoundly than anyone in the twentieth century other than his original mentor, Freud. Probably the best introduction to Jung for a general reader is *Memories, Dreams, Reflections*. Not so much his autobiography as a record of his developing beliefs about himself and the world, the book (first published in the year after his death) describes the spiritual and psychological journey of one remarkable and influential man. According to Jung, 'the sole purpose of human existence is to kindle a light in the darkness of mere being' and his book does just that.

🐦Read on

Man and His Symbols; *The Undiscovered Self*
James Hillman, *The Soul's Code*

HELEN KELLER (1880–1968) USA

THE STORY OF MY LIFE (1902)

There are few more inspirational lives than that of Helen Keller, the deaf and blind American woman who overcame her disabilities to become an internationally respected writer and political activist. Told in her own words, the story of her life and her rescue from isolation by an endlessly patient teacher provides unforgettable evidence that people can triumph against all the odds. Born in Alabama, Helen Keller was struck down by a mysterious illness, possibly scarlet fever or meningitis, at the age of nineteen months which left her deaf, blind and (because she had not learned to speak) mute. Her devastated parents sought some means of drawing their child out of the prison into which her illness had cast her and, with the assistance of Alexander Graham Bell, inventor of the telephone and a pioneer of education for the deaf, they found a young, 20-year-old teacher named Anne Sullivan who agreed to undertake the apparently impossible task of communicating with Helen. The results of the relationship between Anne Sullivan and her charge (a relationship which eventually lasted nearly 50 years) are well known. With astonishing patience on one side and remarkable determination on the other, a teaching programme began which led to Helen Keller becoming the first deafblind person to graduate from college, a bestselling author, a political and social activist and a figure of worldwide fame. The early years of this extraordinary collaboration are recorded in *The Story of My Life*. In a later book Helen Keller wrote, 'If I am happy in spite of my deprivations, if my happiness is so deep that it is a faith, so thoughtful that it becomes a philosophy of life – if, in short, I am an optimist, my testimony to the creed of optimism is worth hearing.' The testimony she provided in *The Story of My Life* certainly continues to be worth reading.

⬃Read on

The World I Live In
Georgina Kleege, *Blind Rage: Letters to Helen Keller*; Oliver Sacks, *Seeing Voices*

READ ON A THEME: INSPIRING MEMOIRS

Karen Armstrong, *The Spiral Staircase*
Andrea Ashworth, *Once in a House on Fire*
Jean-Dominique Bauby, *The Diving-Bell and the Butterfly*
Brian Keenan, *An Evil Cradling*
Frank McCourt, *Angela's Ashes*
Dave Pelzer, *A Child Called It*
Alice Sebold, *Lucky*

JACK KEROUAC (1922–69) USA

ON THE ROAD (1957)

Jack Kerouac was born in Massachusetts into a French-speaking family from Canada. He won a football scholarship to attend Columbia University but Kerouac, sports jock though he was, was always interested in writing and, after dropping out of Columbia, he continued to live in New York where he was able to mix with others who shared his tastes in literature. These friends from the 1940s – people like Allen Ginsberg and William S. Burroughs – became the central figures in the so-called Beat Generation of the next decade and Kerouac, after the publication of *On the Road*, became its king. In his classic account of the Beats' battle against ordinariness, narrator Sal Paradise and his buddy Dean Moriarty (based on Kerouac's charismatic friend Neal Cassady) hit the road and zigzag across the wide open spaces of America in search of love, sex and enlightenment. For Sal, as for his creator, the people who have the most to offer on the road are the ones who refuse to be blinkered by dull conventions and instead are determined to live life to the full. These are the people who are, in Sal's words, 'the mad ones, the ones who are mad to live, mad to talk, mad to be saved, desirous of everything at the same time, the ones that never yawn or say a commonplace thing, but burn, burn, burn like fabulous yellow roman candles exploding like spiders across the stars...' Not everyone found Kerouac's vision of an alternative America compelling and not everyone admired his talents as an author ('This isn't writing, it's typing,' Truman Capote once famously said) but his status as cultural icon is undeniable. Nearly fifty years after its first publication, *On the Road* remains an essential text for rebels both with and without a cause.

⏚Read on
The Dharma Bums; *Visions of Cody*
William S. Burroughs, *Junky*; John Clellon Holmes, *Go*; Hunter S. Thompson, *Fear and Loathing in Las Vegas*

KEN KESEY (1935–2001) USA

ONE FLEW OVER THE CUCKOO'S NEST (1962)
In 1959, Ken Kesey, then a creative writing student at Stanford University, volunteered to act as a guinea pig in a series of medical trials, partly sponsored by the CIA, into the effects of psychoactive drugs like LSD and mescaline. The experiences he had during these trials fed into the novel he was writing and the result was *One Flew Over the Cuckoo's Nest*. Set in a mental hospital in Oregon, the book is narrated by 'Chief' Bromden, a giant American Indian patient there. It tells the story of what happens to the other inmates of the hospital when the drugged routine of their lives is disrupted by the arrival of Randle McMurphy, a larger-than-life prankster who challenges all the rules and assumptions of the establishment. McMurphy is eventually defeated by the powers he sets out to confront but not before he has inspired his fellow patients and given 'Chief' Bromden the incentive to rediscover his true self and escape the hospital. Apart from his fiction –

other novels include *Sometimes a Great Notion and Sailor Song* – Kesey is also known as the leader of the 'Merry Pranksters', the group of proto-hippies who, in the summer of 1964, drove across America in a psychedelically painted school bus, startling the natives of the small towns en route with their appearance and their antics. Throughout his life – and in all his writings – Kesey's aim was to startle. Just as Randle McMurphy strove to awaken his fellow inmates to the world outside the hospital, his creator wanted to stimulate people into new ways of looking at life and its potential. The Merry Pranksters are no more, and their frolics survive only in the pages of *The Electric Kool-Aid Acid Test*, Tom Wolfe's eye-opening and very funny account of travelling with them, but *One Flew Over the Cuckoo's Nest* remains as a testament to Kesey's provocative power.

➽Read on

Sometimes a Great Notion
Gene Brewer, *K-Pax*; Tom Wolfe, *The Electric Kool-Aid Acid Test*

MARTIN LUTHER KING (1929–68) USA

A TESTAMENT OF HOPE (1986)

The most eloquent black leader of the civil rights movement of the 1950s and 1960s was born in Atlanta, Georgia, the son of a Baptist preacher. He went on to become a pastor himself in Montgomery, Alabama and was on hand to accept leadership in one of the first great campaigns for black equality in the USA, the celebrated Montgomery Bus Boycott that began when Rosa Parks refused to give up her seat to a white man. For the rest of his life, King was at the heart of the civil rights movement, delivering hundreds of speeches and playing a major role in demonstrations such as the famous 1963 March on Washington for Jobs and Freedom. In 1964, as the movement's most prominent advocate of non-violent agitation for change, he became the youngest person ever to be awarded the Nobel Peace Prize. Four years later, on 4 April 1968, King was assassinated as he stood on the balcony of a motel room in Memphis. Four decades after his death, his stature as a black leader remains undiminished. Subtitled 'The Essential Writings and Speeches of Martin Luther King Jr', *A Testament of Hope* includes all the most inspiring words that King gave to the world, from his famous 'I Have a Dream' speech to the 'Letter from Birmingham Jail', written in defence of the idea of civil disobedience after he had been arrested for taking part in a non-violent protest against racial segregation. Martin Luther King was a man who believed, in his own words from the 'Letter from Birmingham Jail', that, 'Injustice anywhere is a threat to justice everywhere.' In his own life, so tragically cut short, he campaigned against injustice wherever he found it and the words he wrote and spoke can still move people to take up the battle he fought.

☙Read on

Dietrich Bonhoeffer, *Letter and Papers from Prison*; David Garrow, *Bearing the Cross*; Rosa Parks, *My Story*

BARBARA KINGSOLVER (b. 1955) USA

THE POISONWOOD BIBLE (1999)

Barbara Kingsolver was born and brought up in rural America, the setting for a number of her novels, and studied biology at graduate and postgraduate level. She began to publish her stories in the mid-1980s and has since published close to a dozen volumes of both fiction and non-fiction. Like the great nineteenth-century novelists, Kingsolver clearly believes that fiction has a duty to engage with the real world. She has even sponsored a prize, the Bellwether Prize, which is awarded to a first novel that combines both literary quality and a commitment to literature as a tool for social change. Her own novels are, in the best sense of the word, old-fashioned in that they grapple with political, social and moral issues. In narratives that grip the imaginations of readers, she faces up to concerns about colonialism, the rift between the developed and the undeveloped world, and man's impact on the environment. *The Poisonwood Bible* is her most ambitious novel to date. At its heart is Nathan Price, a narrow-minded Christian evangelist who arrives with his family in the Belgian Congo to serve as a missionary to African people to whom his message means little. The year is 1959 and great changes are on hand but the messianic Price is as blind to these as he is to the real needs of his family and those of the people whose souls he is endeavouring to 'save'. The narrative moves inexorably towards personal tragedy set amid the wider tragedy of a new nation still suffering from the hangover of imperialism. Cleverly and imaginatively told in the very different voices of Price's wife and his four daughters, *The Poisonwood Bible* is a novel that renews confidence in the ability of fiction to confront the major themes of modern life and to illuminate them.

≋Read on

The Bean Trees; *Pigs in Heaven*
Chinua Achebe, *Things Fall Apart*; Jane Smiley, *A Thousand Acres*

NAOMI KLEIN (b. 1970) CANADA

NO LOGO (2000)

If the anti-globalization movement can be said to have a manifesto, then it is probably Naomi Klein's *No Logo*. Her fiery but carefully argued assault on the power of brands opens readers' eyes to the often pernicious ways in which modern capitalism works. From sweatshops in Asia to fast food outlets in America, she examines all the places where people are exploited for profit and shows how we can fight against the exploitation. Naomi Klein was born in Canada, the daughter of a physician and a film-maker who had felt obliged to leave their native America because of their involvement in the anti-Vietnam War movement. She worked as a journalist after university and published *No Logo* when she was still in her twenties. Its success propelled her to worldwide fame as a campaigning intellectual and she has recently published another controversial bestseller, *The Shock Doctrine*, which argues that free market capitalism thrives on and even encourages human disasters. One of the great strengths of Klein's first book is that she recognises the paradoxical ability of giant organisations to appeal to very human desires and she does not underestimate this ability. 'We are looking to brands for poetry and for spirituality,' she writes, 'because we're not getting those things from our communities or from each other.' She understands the power of brands to embody dreams of what life might be and, because of this understanding, she does not dismiss the hold they have on people's lives. Instead, she argues the case for better dreams than those the giant corporations wish to foist upon us. *No Logo* provides both a guide to understanding the process through which brands have come to rule our lives and a handbook to the growing resistance movement which is fighting to curb their power.

☙Read on

The Shock Doctrine
Oliver James, *Affluenza*; George Monbiot, *Captive State*

J. KRISHNAMURTI (1895–1986) INDIA

FREEDOM FROM THE KNOWN (1969)

As a boy, Krishnamurti, the son of an Indian Brahmin, was hailed by leading members of the Theosophical Society as the 'vehicle' of a coming World Teacher and was trained by Annie Besant and other theosophists for the role they thought he was destined to play. When he reached young manhood, the World Teacher-in-waiting disavowed the notion that he was someone special but he continued to travel the world and speak about the life of the mind and the spirit for the rest of his long life. For a man so often acclaimed as a guru himself, Krishnamurti was remarkably dismissive of the very notion that gurus of any kind are of much value. In *Freedom from the Known*, a book of his profoundest thoughts about life, recorded by one of his admirers named Mary Lutyens, he said that, 'you cannot depend on anybody. There is no guide, no teacher, no authority.' To Krishnamurti in his later years, 'The question of whether or not there is a God or truth or reality or whatever you like to call it, can never be answered ... by priests, philosophers or saviours.' Only the individual could ultimately answer the question and he or she could only answer it through self-knowledge. 'Immaturity,' Krishnamurti said, 'lies only in total ignorance of self.' There are many obstacles in the path to self-knowledge. Identifying the self with external forces, whether they be religions, political systems or national institutions, will only postpone the moment when self-knowledge and maturity arrive. If people are able to attain that elusive self-knowledge, then they will be surprised to find that the answers to the most tormenting questions are not only to be found within us but that they are simpler than we tend to think. In the final analysis, Krishnamurti's ideas of what it is to be fully human are remarkably accessible.

⊜Read on

Commentaries on Living (in three volumes); *The First and Last Freedom*

David Bohm, *The Limits of Thought* (discussions between Bohm and Krishnamurti); Sri Ramana Maharshi, *Be As You Are*

MILAN KUNDERA (b. 1929) CZECH REPUBLIC

THE UNBEARABLE LIGHTNESS OF BEING (1984)

Milan Kundera is a Czech novelist whose work fell foul of the old Communist authorities in his native country because of its irony and its unacceptable commitment to ideas of personal and political freedom. His first novel, *The Joke*, immediately established his distinctive voice with its story of a young student whose life is overturned when he makes the mistake of joking about matters that the state and the party consider to be serious. Kundera's most characteristic work of fiction, published after he was encouraged to leave Czechoslovakia and stripped of his Czech nationality, is *The Unbearable Lightness of Being*. The book is set in Prague at the time of the brief flowering of freedom in spring 1968. At its heart is the love affair and marriage between Tomas, a charming but incorrigible womanizer, and Tereza, a woman he meets when she is tending bar in a small town hotel. Tomas, a surgeon, is forced into exile and a menial job by the events of 1968 but continues his obsessive Don Juanism and his relationship with his mistress Sabina, herself entangled in another unhappy affair. *The Unbearable Lightness of Being* is at once an ironic story of the difficulties of sexual and romantic love and a novel of ideas, peppered with aphorisms, short digressions and meditations on the nature of human choice and the effects of mere chance and contingency on our plans and decisions. In an interview, published in *The Paris Review* not long before the publication of his best-known work, Kundera said, 'You can understand nothing about art, particularly modern art, if you do not understand that imagination is a value in itself.' In his fiction he champions the freedom of the imagination with a daring that few other European novelists have matched.

☙Read on

The Joke; *The Book of Laughter and Forgetting*
Bohumil Hrabal, *Closely Observed Trains*; Ivan Klima, *Love and Garbage*

DALAI LAMA (b. 1935) TIBET

THE ART OF HAPPINESS (1998)

To Tibetan Buddhists Tenzin Gyatso is the fourteenth Dalai Lama, the latest in a line of *tulkus* or spiritual masters that stretches back centuries. He was recognised as the reincarnation of the previous Dalai Lama when he was only a small boy and is the temporal as well as the spiritual leader of the Tibetan people. However, since 1959 he has lived in exile in India and his country has been ruled by the People's Republic of China. To other people around the world, including many who do not share his religious views, the Dalai Lama is a man of particular spiritual power and insight. Based on a series of interviews with the psychiatrist Howard Cutler, *The Art of Happiness* is a guide to the kind of everyday problems and troubling questions that face us all. Why are people unhappy? What is romantic love and why is it so often not enough to heal our wounds? How should we respond to evil and to death? The Dalai Lama is not blind to the suffering in the world. How could the leader of a nation that has had a recent history like Tibet's be anything other than acutely aware of, say, the pain that the powerful can inflict upon the powerless? However, he believes that happiness is truly in everybody's grasp. In his speech accepting the 1989 Nobel Peace Prize, he said, 'I believe all suffering is caused by ignorance. People inflict pain on others in the selfish pursuit of their happiness or satisfaction. Yet true happiness comes from a sense of inner peace and contentment, which in turn must be achieved through the cultivation of altruism, of love and compassion and elimination of ignorance, selfishness and greed.' Focusing on the practical application of spiritual values to the difficulties of ordinary life, *The Art of Happiness* draws on the wisdom of one remarkable man to provide a means of attaining that true happiness.

☙Read on

Freedom in Exile
Thich Nhat Hanh, *The Miracle of Mindfulness*; Chogyam Trungpa, *Cutting through Spiritual Materialism*

HARPER LEE (b. 1926) USA

TO KILL A MOCKINGBIRD (1960)

'The one thing that doesn't abide by majority rule is a person's conscience,' says Atticus Finch, the small-town lawyer at the heart of Harper Lee's only novel, and the story demonstrates his determination to live by what he preaches. Seen through the eyes of his daughter, the narrator Scout, Atticus battles against the prejudice and racism that lurks beneath the surface of the town in the Deep South where he practises. He takes on the defence of Tom Robinson, a black man accused of raping a white girl. In the trial, Atticus proves conclusively that the accusation is a false one, based on lies and perjured testimony to the court. Nevertheless, Tom is convicted and is later shot while supposedly attempting to escape from prison. Meanwhile, Scout and her brother Jem learn to develop tolerance and belief in their own convictions as they get to know the truth about Boo Radley, an odd and gentle recluse who has been demonised by most of the townsfolk. Harper Lee was born in the Alabama town of Monroeville and studied law at the University of Alabama. She began to write when she was working in the travel industry in New York and *To Kill a Mockingbird*, begun in the late 1950s, was finally published in the summer of 1960. Its success, both critical and commercial, was instant. It became a bestseller and won the Pulitzer Prize for fiction. Perhaps its success has been too overwhelming for its author because she has published nothing else other than a handful of essays. However, in the forty years and more since its first publication, her novel has become accepted as a classic portrait of a humane man determined to follow his own principles and of a child learning to recognise the injustices of the adult world.

☙Read on

Truman Capote, *Other Voices, Other Rooms* (Harper Lee knew Capote when they were both children in Monroeville and the character of Dill in her novel is usually said to be based on him); William Faulkner, *Intruder in the Dust*; Eudora Welty, *The Optimist's Daughter*

DORIS LESSING (b. 1919) RHODESIA/UK

THE GOLDEN NOTEBOOK (1962)

Doris Lessing was born in Iran, brought up in Rhodesia (now Zimbabwe) and moved to London in 1949 because her involvement in progressive and anti-racist politics made it difficult for her to stay in southern Africa. Her first novel was published the following year and much of her earlier fiction drew upon her experiences in Africa. She is known for two massive and very different sequences of novels. The semi-autobiographical 'Children of Violence' series follows the fortunes of Martha Quest from her childhood in southern Africa to old age in an apocalyptic future; the 'Canopus in Argos' books use the themes and motifs of science fiction to explore a series of possible histories. However, the novel by Doris Lessing which has probably meant most to most readers over the years is *The Golden Notebook*, the story of writer Anna Wulf. The book is set in the 1950s at the height of the Cold War and the Communist Anna is struggling to balance political and personal commitments and to make sense of her experiences of work, sex, love and single parenthood. Anna writes about the different elements of her life in different coloured notebooks. The black notebook records the memories of her past, the red one expresses her political ideas and her interaction with the British Communist Party, the yellow one is for detailing the painful aftermath of an affair, and the blue one for writing down her dreams. It is only in the golden notebook of the title that she can integrate all her different selves into a whole. In one of her notebooks, Anna writes that, 'There is only one real sin, and that is to persuade oneself that the second-best is anything but the second-best'. As a novelist, Lessing has never contented herself with the second-best and *The Golden Notebook* is her most challenging, provoking and inspiring book.

⮒Read on

Martha Quest (and the other books in the 'Children of Violence' sequence); *Memoirs of a Survivor*
Iris Murdoch, *A Severed Head*; Christina Stead, *Letty Fox: Her Luck*

PRIMO LEVI (1919–87) ITALY

IF THIS IS A MAN (1947/1958)

Primo Levi was a Jewish-Italian survivor of Auschwitz. Born in Turin, the city he was to call home for most of his life, Levi studied chemistry at the university there and graduated in 1941. Anti-semitic legislation made it difficult for him to find work but much worse persecution was to follow as the war continued, Mussolini was deposed and Italy became a battleground between Fascist and anti-Fascist forces. Levi joined the Partisans in the hills of northern Italy but was captured by Fascist militia and, as a Jew, was sent to Auschwitz in February 1944. He spent eleven months in the camp, surviving through luck and the small advantages his scientific knowledge conferred on him, before it was liberated by the Red Army. In *If This is a Man* he describes, in clear and careful prose, the terrible events to which he was witness. At times Levi, unsurprisingly, reached the darkest depths of despair and was prepared to give up any hope of survival. The message that another inmate, with his stoic determination to maintain self-respect, gave him was central to his willingness to keep going. This message was that, '... precisely because the Lager was a great machine to reduce us to beasts, we must not become beasts; that even in this place one can survive, and therefore one must want to survive, to tell the story, to bear witness; and that to survive we must force ourselves to save at least the skeleton, the scaffolding, the form of civilization.' Primo Levi did eventually survive to bear witness and he wrote *If This is a Man* soon after the war. The book was eventually published in English in 1958. As a humane testimony to monstrous inhumanity, it has its place among the most important and challenging books of the twentieth century.

⮞Read on

The Drowned and the Saved; *The Periodic Table* (Levi uses the elements of the periodic table as a means of organising a series of auto-biographical essays)
Piera Sonnino, *This Has Happened: An Italian Family in Auschwitz*;
Wladsyslaw Szpilman, *The Pianist*

C.S. LEWIS (1898–1963) UK

SURPRISED BY JOY (1955)

C.S. Lewis spent his career as an academic in Oxford and Cambridge but he is most famous as a writer for children and as one of the twentieth century's most gifted apologists for the Christian faith. His books about the hidden kingdom of Narnia, first published in the 1950s, rapidly became classics of children's literature. His volumes on Christianity include such titles as *Mere Christianity*, *The Problem of Pain* and *The Screwtape Letters*, a clever and mischievous satire in the form of a series of letters of advice supposedly sent by a demon named Screwtape to his nephew Wormwood who is embarking on the tempt-ation of an ordinary man. *A Grief Observed*, originally published under a pseudonym, is a series of moving reflections on grief occasioned by the death of his wife. *Surprised by Joy* is usually described as an autobiography and it does reveal much about Lewis's early life but it is primarily an account of his conversion to Christianity. He does not des-cribe embracing his faith with the fervour usually expected of new devotees. 'In the Trinity Term of 1929 I gave in,' he reports, 'and admitted that God was God, and knelt and prayed: perhaps, that night, the most dejected and reluctant convert in all England.' Yet the reluctant convert had finally found the means of making sense of the 'inconsolable longing' for something elusive which had always haunted him, 'an unsatisfied desire which is itself more desirable than any other satisfaction', to which Lewis attached the untranslatable German word 'Sehnsucht'. For Lewis the something elusive was God and the discovery of faith was the means by which he was 'surprised by joy'. In the book to which he gave that title, he provides one of the most revealing and readable accounts in the twentieth century of a spiritual quest.

≷Read on

A Grief Observed; *The Screwtape Letters*
G.K. Chesterton, *Orthodoxy*; Thomas Merton, *The Seven Storey Mountain*

JAMES LOVELOCK (b. 1919) UK

GAIA (1979)

James Lovelock's long career as a scientist began nearly 70 years ago (he graduated from Manchester University with a degree in chemistry in 1941) and his achievements in a variety of scientific disciplines have been many. His invention of the electron capture detector in the 1950s has proved of lasting benefit in detecting the persistence of certain man-made chemicals in the atmosphere. Others of his inventions have been used in NASA planetary exploration programmes. However, he is best known as the proponent of the 'Gaia' hypothesis, first formulated in the 1960s but brought before a wide audience with the publication in 1979 of his book *Gaia*. (Naming the hypothesis after the Greek goddess of the earth was the suggestion of the novelist William Golding who lived at the time in the same village in Wiltshire as Lovelock.) The hypothesis had its origins in Lovelock's work for the space programme and his efforts to devise methods of detecting life on Mars. He began to speculate on the fundamental differences between lifeless Mars and abundant Earth. He decided that what he termed 'Gaia' was best seen as 'a complex entity involving the Earth's biosphere, atmosphere, oceans, and soil; the totality constituting a feedback or cybernetic system which seeks an optimal physical and chemical environment for life on this planet.' Over the years he has continued to refine and restate his ideas. Many scientists have criticised them but many have come to accept their validity. They remain controversial but Lovelock's vision of an earth that is a self-regulating organism provides powerful support for all of us appalled by our reckless assaults on our planetary environment. His daring new model of the world on which we live has only gained greater relevance in the thirty years since it was first published.

≋Read on

The Ages of Gaia; *The Revenge of Gaia*
Lynn Margulis, *Symbiotic Planet*; Peter Russell, *The Global Brain*; Edward O. Wilson, *The Diversity of Life*

READ ON A THEME: OUR PRECIOUS EARTH

Tim Flannery, *The Weather Makers*
Al Gore, *An Inconvenient Truth*
Elizabeth Kolbert, *Field Notes from a Catastrophe*
Mark Lynas, *Six Degrees*
Bill McGuire, *Surviving Armageddon*
George Monbiot, *Heat: How We Can Stop the Planet Burning*
Fred Pearce, *When the Rivers Run Dry*
Alan Weisman, *The World Without Us*

MALCOLM X (1925–65) USA

THE AUTOBIOGRAPHY OF MALCOLM X (1965)

Malcolm Little was born in Omaha, Nebraska, the son of an African-American Baptist preacher, in 1925. When he was only six, his father was found dead, almost certainly the victim of white vigilantes angered by his support of black politicians and, some years later, his mother, who had never recovered from her loss, was detained in a mental hospital where she was to spend the rest of her life. Malcolm drifted into crime and addiction and was imprisoned for ten years in 1946. In prison, he became a Black Muslim and, once released, he reinvented himself as a powerful advocate of black power and black separatism. He was soon renowned as a magnetically powerful public speaker. In 1964, after a pilgrimage to Mecca, he announced his rejection of his separatist beliefs and his new found conviction that good men of all races could join together to combat discrimination and injustice. On 21 February 1965, Malcolm X was speaking at the Audubon Ballroom in New York when he was shot several times by men who rose from their seats in the audience and rushed the podium. He was pronounced dead on arrival at a nearby hospital. Although three men were eventually convicted of his assassination, controversy about who really shot Malcolm X continues to this day. Whoever was guilty had killed one of the most remarkable Americans of his generation as his auto-biography demonstrates. Written by Alex Haley, and based on long interviews with Malcolm X in the year before he was assassinated, the book is a blazingly honest account of Malcolm's life in crime, his conversion to Islam (the undoubted turning point in his life) and the spiritual and intellectual journey he had made. It is one of the most powerful and revelatory documents to emerge from 1950s and 1960s America and from the movement to fight racism and oppression.

≋Read on

Malcolm X Speaks (a selection from his speeches)
James Weldon Johnson, *The Autobiography of an Ex-Colored Man*;
Richard Wright, *Black Boy*

NELSON MANDELA (b. 1918) SOUTH AFRICA

LONG WALK TO FREEDOM

Born into a high-status family in the Transkei, Nelson Mandela trained as a lawyer and joined the African National Congress in 1944. He campaigned against the racial segregation of apartheid from its introduction into South Africa in 1948 and endured several periods of imprisonment before he was given a life sentence in 1964. He remained in jail for 26 years, an increasingly potent symbol of resistance to apartheid. Released in 1990, he became the first black president of South Africa four years later, guiding the country in its transition from minority rule to true democracy. *Long Walk to Freedom* is the personal testament of one of the moral and political giants of the twentieth century, and charts Mandela's journey from prison to presidency of a new, apartheid-free South Africa. His enduring faith, through years of hardship and imprisonment, that truth and justice could eventually triumph over oppression is humbling. So, too, is his conviction that love is ultimately a more powerful force in the world than hate. 'No one is born hating another person because of the colour of his skin, or his background, or his religion,' he writes. 'People must learn to hate, and if they can learn to hate, they can be taught to love, for love comes more naturally to the human heart than its opposite.' Given the story of Mandela's life, his hard-won belief carries a credibility that readers cannot fail to find moving.

⊜Read on

Anthony Sampson, *Mandela: The Authorised Biography*; Desmond Tutu, *The Rainbow People of God*; Donald Woods, *Biko*

NADEZHDA MANDELSTAM (1899–1980) RUSSIA

HOPE AGAINST HOPE (1970)

The first of Nadezhda Mandelstam's two harrowing but ultimately uplifting memoirs of life in Stalinist Russia records the persecution she and her husband, the poet Osip Mandelstam, endured. There is an untranslatable pun embedded in the title of the memoir and its successor, *Hope Abandoned*. The author's first name, 'Nadezhda', means 'hope' in Russian and, despite the title of the second volume, the reader can take a strange kind of hope from Mandelstam's writings. From the tragic story of the destruction she witnessed and of her husband's slow disintegration and death, she succeeds in creating a masterpiece that bears witness to the ultimate triumph of creativity and the liberated human spirit. Osip Mandelstam was already a renowned poet in revolutionary Russia when he married a young Jewish woman named Nadezhda Hazin in 1921. Throughout the 1920s and early 1930s, his literary fame continued to grow but Mandelstam was constitutionally incapable of the kind of conformism required of writers in the Soviet era. This was demonstrated most dangerously in 1933 when he wrote what has been described as 'a sixteen-line death sentence' – an acerbically satirical poem criticising Stalin. Mandelstam was not immediately arrested but, within a year, he had been despatched into exile and the last years of his life were made wretched by harrassment and persecution. He died while in transit to a labour camp after he had been sentenced to imprisonment for 'counter-revolutionary activities'. In his wife's memoir his death becomes somehow emblematic of all the suffering endured by the Russian people during the years of Stalin's 'Great Terror'. 'If nothing else is left, one must scream,' Nadezhda

Mandelstam wrote. 'Silence is the real crime against humanity.' Her extraordinary book represents her refusal to acquiesce in such a crime.

⮂Read on
Hope Abandoned
Evgenia Ginzburg, *Into the Whirlwind*; Varlam Shalamov, *Kolyma Tales*

GABRIEL GARCIA MARQUEZ (b. 1928)
COLOMBIA

ONE HUNDRED YEARS OF SOLITUDE (1967/1970)
South America's most admired novelist and winner of the Nobel Prize for Literature in 1982, Gabriel Garcia Marquez began his career as a journalist. His first stories, published in Spanish the mid-1950s, introduced the imaginary town of Macondo which has been the setting for much of his fiction, including his most famous novel, *One Hundred Years of Solitude*. In its opening chapter, as Colonel Aureliano Buendia faces a firing squad, the extraordinary history of generations of his family unfolds in his mind. They begin as poor peasants in a one-roomed hut on the edge of a swamp. They proliferate wildly until the existence of the family and the existence of Macondo seem indissolubly linked. Then, led by the Colonel, they defend the old values of the town against invasion by a government which wants to impose the same laws on Macondo as everywhere else. Finally, the dynasty disappears from reality, living on only in fantasy, as a memory of how human beings

were before the world changed. Macondo is a town unlike any other and its people, both the Buendias and others, live in the mind like few other fictional characters. When the technological wonders of the modern age reach Macondo, the townsfolk are unsure what to make of them. 'It was as if God had decided to put to the test every capacity for surprise,' Marquez writes, 'and was keeping the inhabitants of Macondo in a permanent alternation between excitement and disappointment, doubt and revelation, to such an extreme that no one knew for certain where the limits of reality lay.' In the pages of his masterpiece it is equally difficult to judge where the limits of reality lie. Possible and impossible events intertwine, time dissolves and imagination takes precedence in a narrative that renews the potential of fiction to re-invent the world.

See also: *100 Must-Read Books for Men*

⮧Read on

Chronicle of a Death Foretold; *The General in his Labyrinth*
Augusto Roa Bastos, *I, the Supreme*; Mario Vargas Llosa, *The War of the End of the World*

YANN MARTEL (b. 1963) SPAIN/CANADA

LIFE OF PI (2001)

Born in Spain of Canadian parents, Yann Martel had a peripatetic childhood and youth, spending time in countries as diverse as Costa Rica and Iran, France and India. He has continued to travel widely as an adult. He studied philosophy at university in Canada and became a full-time writer in his late twenties. His first book, a collection of short stories entitled *The Facts Behind the Helsinki Roccamatios*, was published in 1993 and was followed three years later by *Self*, an ambitious novel about shifting sexual identities. Both books won some praise from critics but this was as nothing compared to the acclaim that met his second novel, *Life of Pi* which went on to win the 2002 Booker Prize. The award of the Booker was certainly justified. The book is one of the more extraordinary and inventive works of fiction to appear so far in the twenty-first century. Martel clearly has confidence in the straightforward power of story-telling but he also demonstrates belief in the ability of the novel to bear the weight of philosophical speculation and digression as well. Even the briefest precis of the plot gives some indication of how unusual the book is. Teenage Piscine ('Pi') Patel, while attempting to travel from India to a new life in Canada, becomes the sole human survivor of the wreck of a cargo ship in the Pacific. Sharing a lifeboat with an assortment of animal survivors of the shipwreck, including a zebra, a hyena, an orang-utan and a 450-pound Bengal tiger named Richard Parker, he has time to ponder his fate and his future as the makeshift ark drifts across the ocean towards a landfall. Unique and uncategorisable, Martel's novel mingles elements of old-fashioned adventure stories with meditations on the nature of faith and the value of religion.

⮑Read on
The Facts Behind the Helsinki Roccamatios; *Self*
Daniel Defoe, *Robinson Crusoe*; Mark Haddon, *The Curious Incident of the Dog in the Night-time*

ANNE MICHAELS (b. 1958) CANADA

FUGITIVE PIECES (1997)

Before the publication of *Fugitive Pieces*, the Canadian writer Anne Michaels was known as a poet and the language of her first novel is charged with the resonance and memorable imagery of the finest poetry. At its heart is the story of Jakob Beer. At the beginning of the novel, Jakob is a small boy who has fled the Nazis and the scene of his parents' murder and is in hiding in the forests of Poland. Covered in mud and filth, he is discovered by Athos Roussos, a Greek scholar excavating the ancient Polish city of Biskupin. Athos takes responsibility for the boy and smuggles him out of Poland and back to his home on the Greek island of Zakynthos. As Jakob grows up, Athos becomes his beloved mentor, who introduces him to the pleasures of knowledge and language and intellectual curiosity but the young man remains haunted by his loss and, especially, by fleeting memories of a sister whose final fate he has never learned. The narrative continues to follow Jakob as he moves from Europe to Canada and back again, charting the failure of his marriage, his attempts to come to terms with his extraordinary past and his short-lived happiness with a much younger woman. Through the story of Jakob and those whose lives he affects, Anne Michaels explores difficult ideas about the wounds that history inflicts on people and the ways in which even the worst of them can be healed. 'Hold a book in your hand,' Jakob says at one point in the novel, citing an old Hebrew saying, 'and you're a pilgrim at the gates of a new city.' Entering the new city that is *Fugitive Pieces* is an experience that lingers long in the memory.

⮞Read on

Cynthia Ozick, *The Shawl*; Bernhard Schlink, *The Reader*; Rachel Seiffert, *The Dark Room*

ALICE MILLER (b. 1923) POLAND/SWITZERLAND

THE DRAMA OF THE GIFTED CHILD (1979/1981)

Alice Miller is a psychologist and psychotherapist who was born in Poland and moved to Switzerland as a young woman soon after the end of the Second World War. She studied at the University of Basel, gaining a PhD in 1953, and then worked as a psychoanalyst for more than twenty years. In the 1970s, she began publishing a series of powerful indictments of traditional methods of raising children, arguing that the child's well-being is regularly sacrificed to the interests of the parents. A 'poisonous pedagogy' is too often used which damages the emotional development of the child. Miller has written about extreme examples of this – in her book *For Your Own Good*, for example, she analyses the upbringings of Hitler and of serial killers – but her argument is that 'poisonous pedagogy' permeates society and that the many children who suffer from it carry its effects with them through their entire lives. The trauma of any kind of abuse in childhood – physical, sexual or emotional – is longlasting. If parents, for whatever reasons, refuse to acknowledge children as individuals, then the consequences are terrible. 'A little reflection soon shows,' she writes in *The Drama of the Gifted Child*, her first and still her most famous book, 'how inconceivable it is really to love others (not merely to need them), if one cannot love oneself as one really is. And how could a person do that if, from the very beginning, he has had no chance to experience his true feelings and to learn to know himself?' Miller writes movingly about the ways in which childhood can become a prison for the real self but she also offers hope that people can recover lost feelings and repressed histories and thus free themselves from the chains of the past.

➳Read on

For Your Own Good; *Thou Shalt Not Be Aware*
Susan Forward, *Toxic Parents*

READ ON A THEME: THE CHILD IS FATHER TO THE MAN

Virginia M. Axline, *Dibs In Search of Self*
John Bowlby, *A Secure Base*
Margaret Donaldson, *Children's Minds*
Erik H. Erikson, *Childhood and Society*
John Holt, *How Children Learn*
Jean Liedloff, *The Continuum Concept*
Neil Postman, *The Disappearance of Childhood*
D.W. Winnicott, *The Child, the Family and the Outside World*

DAN MILLMAN (b. 1946) USA

THE WAY OF THE PEACEFUL WARRIOR (1980)

Dan Millman was a world champion when he was still in his teens, taking first place in the World Trampoline Championship in London in 1964 but early success only marked the beginning of a long spiritual quest which he has chronicled in his books, the best known of which remains *The Way of the Peaceful Warrior*. Cast in the form of thinly disguised fiction, *The Way of the Peaceful Warrior* has a central character named Dan who meets a mysterious mentor he dubs 'Socrates' working at a gas station. Socrates has a wisdom that Dan can only admire and he passes on to the younger man his perceptions about the world and about the real nature of success in it. The old gas attendant has no easy answers. The world is a difficult place. As Socrates says, 'If you don't get what you want, you suffer; if you get what you don't want, you suffer; even when you get exactly what you want, you still suffer because you can't hold on to it forever.' However, it is the mind that is the predicament because it 'wants to be free of change. Free of pain, free of the obligations of life and death.' The only way to escape the chains of this way of thinking is to accept that 'change is a law, and no amount of pretending will alter that reality'. Once he has learned that essential truth, Dan is able to embark on the odyssey which transforms him into a 'peaceful warrior', living in the moment and taking pleasure in it. Confidently sub-titled 'A Book That Changes Lives', *The Way of the Peaceful Warrior* has done exactly what it claims to do for many people. Through its intriguing blend of fact and fiction, and through the character of Socrates, it leads readers on a memorable journey.

≋Read on

The Life You Were Born to Live; *Sacred Journey of the Peaceful Warrior*

Louise Hay, *You Can Heal Your Life*; Anthony Robbins, *Awaken the Giant Within*; Robin S. Sharma, *The Monk Who Sold His Ferrari*; Eckhart Tolle, *The Power of Now*

READ ON A THEME: IT'S ALL IN THE PSYCHOLOGY

Eric Berne, *Games People Play*
Dale Carnegie, *How to Win Friends and Influence People*
Mihaly Csikszentmihalyi, *Flow*
Clarissa Pinkola Estes, *Women Who Run with Wolves*
Shakti Gawain, *Creative Visualization*
John Gray, *Men Are from Mars, Women Are from Venus*
Susan Jeffers, *Feel the Fear and Do It Anyway*
Robin Norwood, *Women Who Love Too Much*
Gail Sheehy, *Passages*
Robin Skynner & John Cleese, *Families and How to Survive Them*

TONI MORRISON (b. 1931) USA

BELOVED (1987)

In the fiction she has published over the last four decades, Toni Morrison, winner of the 1993 Nobel Prize for Literature, has shown herself to be one of the most profound and imaginative of all interpreters of the black American experience. Her novels have ranged from the story of a black girl obsessed by white standards of beauty

(*The Bluest Eye*) to an enigmatic exploration of racial and cultural tension focused on an all-black township in Oklahoma (*Paradise*). However, her finest work is usually acknowledged to be **Beloved**. Loosely based on the real-life story of Margaret Garner, an escaped slave who killed her own daughter rather than see her returned to slavery, this is the tale of Sethe who, when the novel opens in the year 1873, is living in a house near Cincinatti with her daughter Denver. Sethe harbours terrible memories of events years earlier when she escaped from her brutal life as slave to a sadist. Her freedom was short-lived and, when she was tracked down and recaptured, she tried to kill all four of her children. Only a baby girl died and now, eighteen years later, it seems that the ghost of that child has returned in the enigmatic shape of 'Beloved', a young girl who represents not only Sethe's lost child but all the cruel legacy of slavery. Moving back and forth in time, and flitting between the viewpoints of several different characters, *Beloved* is a complicated but compelling narrative that brings the dehumanising consequences of slavery vividly to life. All the characters are haunted by the ghosts of history and Morrison provides no easy healing for the damage they have all suffered. Her novel looks at African-American history with unblinkered eyes and presents it to the reader with a complete lack of sentimentality.

≋Read on

Paradise; *Song of Solomon*

Charles Johnson, *Middle Passage*; Steven Weisenburger, *Modern Medea* (historical study of the Margaret Garner case)

FRIEDRICH NIETZSCHE (1844–1900) GERMANY

THUS SPOKE ZARATHUSTRA (1883–85/1909)

Nietzsche was born in a small town in Saxony where his father was the Lutheran pastor and he was educated at the Schulpforta, a famous German boarding school, and at the universities of Bonn and Leipzig. He was a brilliant classical scholar and was offered a professorship at a Swiss university when still only in his twenties. His university career lasted for a decade until it was brought to an end by his ill health. He then began a nomadic life, moving from city to city across Europe and surviving as an independent scholar and writer. In 1889, while in Turin, he suffered what was to be a permanent breakdown of his mental health which left him an invalid in the care of his sister for the rest of his life. Nietzsche was not, in any sense, a systematic philosopher, rigorously pursuing an argument. His ideas emerge in a sequence of devastatingly precise and resonant aphorisms and insights which move swiftly from subject to subject, from art and music to science and morality. He challenged most of the ruling assumptions and ideas of his time. He rejected Christianity, with its emphasis on humility and submission to an objectively existing God, as the morality of the slave. Instead he believed in an extreme form of subjective idealism: that we live in a self-created world which is the projection of our own minds. There is no objectively existing 'reality' beyond the creative powers of the human will. Probably no great philosopher has been so misunderstood as Nietzsche. His ideas have been seized upon and twisted out of recognition by later generations, most damagingly for his reputation by the Nazis. However, it is also true to say that no other great philosopher can speak so directly and challengingly to ordinary readers. Read a book like *Thus Spoke Zarathustra* and the world will never seem quite the same again.

⮒Read on

Beyond Good and Evil; *Ecce Homo*
Walter Benjamin, *Illuminations*; Elias Canetti, *Crowds and Power*; Arthur Schopenhauer, *Essays and Aphorisms*

MICHAEL ONDAATJE (b. 1943) SRI LANKA/ CANADA

THE ENGLISH PATIENT (1992)

Born in Sri Lanka, Michael Ondaatje spent his childhood there and in England and then moved to Canada as a young man. After studying in Toronto and Kingston, Ontario, he became a university lecturer in English literature and a poet. When he started to write fiction, it was in a prose that was as rich, dense and allusive as his verse. Early, experimental novels like *Coming Through Slaughter* and *The Collected Works of Billy the Kid* won him admirers but it was only with the publication of *The English Patient*, which won the Booker Prize and was later transformed by Anthony Minghella into a successful film, that Ondaatje gained a much wider audience. Written in a prose that lingers on the details of the visible world and unfolding its story in a complex jigsaw of interlocking scenes, the novel is a compelling exploration of love, memory and desire. As the Second World War drags to its conclusion, a nurse and her patient, an Englishman burnt beyond recognition and swathed in bandages, are holed up in a villa near Florence after the retreat of the Germans. Two other damaged individuals, a Sikh bomb disposal expert and a former criminal who has suffered torture, are now the villa's only other occupants. As the nurse and her two companions enter into complex relationships of their own and speculate about the enigma of the English patient, he returns in his own mind to North Africa before the war and to memories of an intense but doomed love affair. In *The English Patient*, narrative provides the bare bones on which Ondaatje hangs his often haunting and beautiful language and imagery. The novel stays in the memory long after it has been read, a reminder of just how poignant and enigmatic fiction can be.

📖**Read on**

Anil's Ghost
Paul Bowles, *The Sheltering Sky*; D.M. Thomas, *The White Hotel*

BORIS PASTERNAK (1890–1960) RUSSIA

DR. ZHIVAGO (1958)

In Russia, Pasternak is best known as a poet; in the West, readers know him for his novel *Dr. Zhivago* which provoked a savage response from the Soviet authorities of the time. They banned the book and made him renounce the Nobel Prize he was awarded in 1958, the same year the first British edition of his masterpiece appeared. Pasternak's powerful and gripping novel follows the doomed love affair of an idealistic poet and doctor, Yuri Zhivago, and a teacher, Lara, as it is played out against the epic backdrop of the Russian Revolution and Civil War. In the story of these two people caught up in world-changing historical events, human emotions of love and generosity are championed in a time when hatred, division and violence have taken hold. 'The whole human way of life has been destroyed and ruined,' Lara says at one point in the novel. 'All that's left is the bare, shivering human soul, stripped to the last shred, the naked force of the human psyche for which nothing has changed because it was always cold and shivering and reaching out to its nearest neighbour, as cold and lonely as itself.' Neither Zhivago nor Lara survive the events chronicled in the novel. After enduring much in his service as a medical officer in Tsarist and revolutionary armies, he dies of a heart attack in Moscow. She disappears from the novel and from history, probably a victim (although it is never explicitly stated) of State terrorism. Yet their love, enjoyed in the few snatched moments that history allows them, somehow transcends their deaths. Despite all the suffering and the pain that Pasternak's narrative records, it is the love between them and the human emotions they embody that readers remember and that Pasternak invites us to celebrate.

≋Read on

The Last Summer
Mikhail Bulgakov, *The White Guard*; Leo Tolstoy, *War and Peace*

M. SCOTT PECK (1936–2005) USA

THE ROAD LESS TRAVELLED (1978)

Born in New York City, M. Scott Peck studied at Harvard and then served for a decade as a psychiatrist in the US Army. After a further ten years in private practice, he was in a position to redirect his energies towards working as an inspirational speaker. The means for doing this were provided by *The Road Less Travelled*, first published in 1978 but a bestseller throughout the 1980s and beyond. Many self-help gurus gain their successes by offering apparently pain-free ways to achieve all that potential disciples have dreamed of achieving. Scott Peck is not that kind of guru. 'Life is difficult,' he states in the famous opening sentence of *The Road Less Travelled*. 'This is a great truth,' he continues, 'one of the greatest truths. It is a great truth because once we truly see this truth, we transcend it. Once we truly know that life is difficult – once we truly understand and accept it – then life is no longer difficult. Because once it is accepted, the fact that life is difficult no longer matters.' Paradoxically it is probably because of the author's refusal to don rose-tinted glasses that his book has had the success it has had. Honesty and the admission that there is no easy path to happiness and enlightenment have their own attractions. Peck believes that people are only too likely to turn their backs on responsibility and opportunities to embrace real freedom. Many will refuse to change and the road to a richer life is, indeed, the road less travelled. However, for those prepared to take it, the rewards are substantial. Peck's books – 'self-help books that are read by people who don't read self-help books', as one admirer described them – are essential guides to the journey along the road.

⪜Read on

Further Along the Road Less Travelled; *People of the Lie*
Harold Kushner, *When Bad Things Happen to Good People*; Thomas
Moore, *Care of the Soul*

STEVEN PINKER (b. 1954) CANADA

HOW THE MIND WORKS

Why do our minds work in the ways that they do? There can be few more
intriguing questions we can ask ourselves and, over the last fifteen
years, the Canadian academic Steven Pinker has done more than
almost anybody to provide general readers with answers to it. Before
the publication of *The Language Instinct* in 1994, Pinker was already
well-known in his field as an innovative thinker on the development of
language in children. His much-praised first book for a general
readership brought his ideas to a wider public. In it he argues that the
capacity for language is imprinted in the biological structure of our
brains and develops spontaneously in the growing child. Language is
an instinct. People know how to talk in the same way that spiders know
how to spin webs or eagles know how to fly. His second book was more
ambitious as its title suggests. In *How the Mind Works* he extends his
approach to language to cover all the functions of the mind from vision
to memory, consciousness to the emotions. Drawing on scientific
disciplines like cognitive science and (particularly) evolutionary
psychology, Pinker advances a model of the human mind that com-

bines the theory of computation and Darwinian evolution. And, along the way, he gives answers to such unexpected questions as why a man's salary tends to increase as his height does and what happens when we fall in love. The subjects that Pinker tackles are weighty ones but he writes about them with a lightness and a clarity that make even the most difficult of concepts comprehensible to non-specialists. *How the Mind Works* (and his later volumes like *The Blank Slate*) allow us all to enter cutting-edge scientific debates about human nature and the human mind.

⮃Read on

The Blank Slate; *The Language Instinct*; *The Stuff of Thought*
Antonio C. Damasio, *The Feeling of What Happens*; Robert Wright, *The Moral Animal*

ROBERT M. PIRSIG (b. 1928) USA

ZEN AND THE ART OF MOTORCYCLE MAINTENANCE (1974)

Growing up in Minnesota, Robert Pirsig was a gifted child with an unusually high IQ who gained a place to study biochemistry at university when he was still only in his mid-teens. As an adult he struggled at first to find his way in life. He served with the US military in Korea where he developed an interest in Buddhism and, on his return to the US, he became a teacher and lecturer. In his early thirties, he suffered a breakdown which resulted in his spending time in a mental hospital where he underwent electric shock therapy. When *Zen and the Art of Motorcycle Maintenance* was first published, it was immediately recognised as utterly original and memorable, a book that attempts to blend Eastern and Western thought into a unique and uncategorisable whole. At its simplest, Pirsig's narrative is the story of a motorcycle trip he takes across America, accompanied by his young son, but there is much more to it than first appears. At its heart, however, is his vision of a world where the rationality of the West and the non-intellectual insights of the East can be reconciled. To Pirsig, the two are not necessarily in conflict. 'The Buddha,' he writes, 'resides as comfortably in the circuits of a digital computer or the gears of a cycle transmission as he does at the top of a mountain or in the petals of a flower.' Reason and logic, as represented by the motorcycle and its maintenance, are important but so too are the intuition and creativity, represented by the Buddha. Robert Pirsig turns the trip he and his son make into a personal odyssey in search of what is true, real and valuable in life. Striving to heal the age-old division between science and mysticism, he creates a philosophical masterpiece.

≋Read on

Lila: An Inquiry into Morals (more of Pirsig's ideas about what he calls a 'Metaphysics of Quality')

William Least-Heat Moon, *Blue Highways*; Peter Matthiessen, *The Snow Leopard*; Ted Simon, *Jupiter's Travels*

SYLVIA PLATH (1932–63) USA

THE BELL JAR (1963)

Sylvia Plath, remembered as much for her difficult relationship with the late Poet Laureate Ted Hughes and for her suicide as she is for her poetry, also wrote a semi-autobiographical novel, first published under a pseudonym a month before her death. *The Bell Jar* tells the story of Esther Greenwood, a brilliant young college student who is given the chance to work in the exhilarating world of New York journalism. The year is 1953 and ideas of femininity and the correct social roles for women are in flux. Esther is torn between rebellion and conformity, between her ambitions to excel as a writer and a nagging wish simply to succumb to convention and marry her boyfriend Buddy. She realises that she has been handed a golden opportunity but she seems unable to take full advantage of it. She feels alienated from the excitements of city life and this feeling only increases when she fails to win acceptance on a prestigious writing course and is obliged to return to suburban life for the summer. The narrative charts Esther's descent into profound depression, her attempt at suicide, her treatment in hospital and her eventual return, through time and therapy, to the ordinary world. Plath's novel takes as its subject some of the bleakest feelings that a person can endure. Her sense of misery and separation from the world makes Esther feel like she is trapped under a laboratory bell jar, deprived of all air. She struggles to make any connection with reality. 'To the person in the bell jar, blank and stopped as a dead baby,' as it says in the novel, 'the world itself is the bad dream.' Yet the novel is not, in the final analysis, a depressing one. At the end of the book, Esther's renewed ability to function in the world, however compromised and threatened by the unknown future it is, seems like a kind of triumph.

⫯Read on

Johnny Panic and the Bible of Dreams; *Letters Home*
Susanna Kaysen, *Girl, Interrupted*; Elizabeth Wurtzel, *Prozac Nation*

ANNIE PROULX (b. 1935) USA

THE SHIPPING NEWS (1993)

Annie Proulx did not begin publishing fiction until she was in her fifties but her original (often dark) imagination, her evocative use of landscape and setting, her quirky humour and arresting use of language brought her swift success. Today, she is probably best known for 'Brokeback Mountain', a poignant story of two Wyoming ranch-hands drawn into an unexpected and intense sexual relationship. However, before the Hollywood movie version made that novella famous, she gained attention (and the Pulitzer Prize) with her full-length novel, *The Shipping News*. At the beginning of the book, the central character Quoyle is an unsuccessful newspaperman in New York, still brooding on the humiliations of his marriage to a woman who first betrayed him and then was killed in an accident, leaving him with two small children. Accompanied by his young daughters and by a formidable maiden aunt, he returns to Newfoundland, his father's birthplace, and there he finds the fulfilment that eluded him in the city.

He establishes himself at the local newspaper, finds himself drawn into the daily life of the community and emerges from the protective shell of loneliness to begin a new and rewarding relationship. More optimistic about human possibility than much of Proulx's other work, *The Shipping News* is saved from the banality an outline of its plot might suggest by her wit, originality and skilful unravelling of events. Quoyle's transformation becomes an offbeat celebration of the potential people have for change. As Proulx, in the charged and poetic language she employs to such great effect in *The Shipping News*, says, 'Water may be older than light, diamonds crack in hot goat's blood, mountaintops give off cold fire, forests appear in mid-ocean; it may happen that a crab is caught with the shadow of a hand on its back, and that the wind be imprisoned in a bit of knotted string. And it may be that love sometimes occurs without pain or misery.'

ᴥRead on
Accordion Crimes; *Close Range* (a collection of short stories that includes the well-known novella 'Brokeback Mountain')
Marilynne Robinson, *Gilead*; Richard Russo, *Empire Falls*

JAMES REDFIELD (b. 1950) USA

THE CELESTINE PROPHECY (1993)
James Redfield, a therapist who had quit his job to work as a writer, could scarcely have imagined what the future was to hold when he self-

published *The Celestine Prophecy* in 1993. He began by selling it into bookshops himself but its word-of-mouth success was such that the rights were bought by a major publisher and Redfield's blend of adventure narrative and self-help book ('half Indiana Jones and half Scott Peck', as one reviewer described it) became one of the biggest bestsellers of the 1990s. *The Celestine Prophecy* is presented as a novel. In the rain forests of Peru an ancient manuscript has been discovered. In its pages are nine insights into the nature and meaning of life. The narrator of the story decides to head for South America to learn more of the manuscript and its spiritual truths but he discovers that the powers that be, in both state and Church, are disturbed by the idea that the insights will be further disseminated and are prepared to go to great lengths to stop this. As the narrator learns each insight, one by one, and sees each one begin to operate in his life, he is also obliged to escape the dangerous attentions of those who wish to keep the insights to themselves. The story of *The Celestine Prophecy* is not always a particularly compelling one nor its characters particularly convincing. Redfield is no great novelist and his novel is intended primarily as a vehicle for the nine insights. These begin with the awareness that a new spiritual awakening is underway and that individuals can only achieve their full potential if they align themselves with it. From this basis, they move towards the revelation of how humans can evolve into a new dimension of existence. Sophisticated sceptics may mock *The Celestine Prophecy* but, as its startling word-of-mouth success indicates, it speaks very directly to millions of people.

≋Read on

The Tenth Insight; *The Secret of Shambhala*

Mitch Albom, *The Five People You Meet in Heaven*; Neale Donald Walsch, *Conversations with God*

LUKE RHINEHART (b. 1932) USA

THE DICE MAN (1971)

A bored and unhappy psychiatrist named Luke Rhinehart has a moment of revelation. He decides that, in future, he will make no conscious decisions about his life. Instead, he will allow the fall of the dice to determine his actions. He will merely put forward options and then let the dice choose between them. By this simple means he will shake himself out of the inertia and the tedium which have come to dominate his life. As he says, looking back on his experiment, 'breaking my established patterns was threatening to my deeply ingrained selves and pricked me to a level of consciousness which is unusual, unusual since the whole instinct of human behavior is to find environments congenial to the relaxation of consciousness. By creating problems for myself I created thought.' As he goes on to acknowledge, 'I also created problems'. *The Dice Man* chronicles, with deadpan humour, the freedoms and the problems that rolling the dice brings to Rhinehart's life. Appropriately for a novel so enthralled by the mysteries of chance and randomness, its author remains an enigma. Is he really a psychiatrist named Luke Rhinehart? Or is he George Cockroft, sometime psychologist and university teacher? Could he even be H.F. Saint, author of a book called *Memoirs of an Invisible Man*? No one seems sure. What is certain is that *The Dice Man* is a novel like few others – a subversive, scary and liberating exploration of what life might be like if it was guided by the throw of a dice. Some of the earlier editions of the novel carried the confident tagline that, 'This book can change your life.' It's a claim made by publishers on behalf of many books but, when applied to *The Dice Man*, it may just be true.

❧Read on
The Search for the Dice Man
Chuck Palahniuk, *Fight Club*; H.F. Saint, *Memoirs of an Invisible Man*; Nassim Nicholas Taleb, *The Black Swan* (a non-fiction investigation of the power of unpredictability in our lives)

SOGYAL RINPOCHE (b. 1950?) TIBET

THE TIBETAN BOOK OF LIVING AND DYING (1992)
Born in eastern Tibet and recognised at an early age as the reincarnation of a famous Buddhist teacher, Sogyal Rinpoche grew up in the mountainous Indian state of Sikkim and went on to study at university in Delhi before travelling to the West in the early 1970s. For the last thirty years he has been one of the most prominent interpreters of Buddhism to Western audiences, both through his writings and through the international organisation he founded and called Rigpa.

The Tibetan Book of Living and Dying, which has been a bestseller in a number of different European languages, provides a wide-ranging survey of Tibetan Buddhist ideas about the present life and the life (or lives) to come. To Western minds, the experience of dying is often seen as one that is too anxiety-provoking to contemplate. To Rinpoche and other Buddhists, it is only through contemplation of death that the joys of life can be revealed. 'When we finally know we are dying', Rinpoche writes, 'and all other sentient beings are dying with us, we start to have a burning, almost heartbreaking sense of the fragility and preciousness of each moment and each being, and from this can grow a deep, clear, limitless compassion for all beings.' Paradoxically to Western eyes, the contemplation of death opens the gate to a fuller life. In his book, Rinpoche explains ideas of karma and rebirth which are central to a specifically Buddhist tradition but much of what he writes about the value of the impermanent world in which we presently find ourselves, about the nature of spirituality and the best means to nurture it, is applicable to the lives of us all. *The Tibetan Book of Living and Dying* can help people of many faiths and none to understand the meaning of life and the place of death within it.

≋Read on

The Future of Buddhism
The Tibetan Book of the Dead
Walpola Rahula, *What the Buddha Taught*

J.K. ROWLING (b. 1965) UK

HARRY POTTER AND THE PHILOSOPHER'S STONE (1997)

It is difficult to believe that, only a little over a decade ago, the names of Harry Potter, Hermione Granger and Ron Weasley were unknown and Hogwarts School of Witchcraft and Wizardry was not a familiar location to millions and millions of children (and adults) around the world. So enormous has been the success of J.K. Rowling's books and the films that have followed them that the characters seem to have been around for ever. Her own story – her journey from struggling single mother to her present position as one of the richest and bestselling authors of all time – seems like a contemporary fairy story. And the novel with which she first made her mark is a tale of magical transformations and hidden powers suddenly revealed. When we are first introduced to our hero in *Harry Potter and the Philosopher's Stone* he is a nobody, sleeping under the stairs in a house where he is unwelcome. Harry, of course, has secrets of which even he knows nothing and it is not long before the poor relative has been whisked away from the Dursleys and sent to Hogwarts. There he meets new friends, tests out his skills as a wizard and learns just a little of the destiny which will pit him against Lord Voldemort in a titanic struggle of good against evil. There is no doubt about the status of the Harry Potter volumes as life-changing books for many people. Rowling's impact on young readers has been incalculable. No writer has done more to inspire young readers with a love for fiction than she has and the first adventure of her bespectacled would-be wizard introduces him (and us) to Hogwarts, the most extraordinary school in the world, and to the assortment of beguiling characters who spend their time there.

➥Read on

Harry Potter and the Chamber of Secrets; *Harry Potter and the Prisoner of Azkaban* (the next two titles in the series of seven books in all)
Michael Ende, *The Neverending Story*; Philip Pullman, *Northern Lights* (the first in the *His Dark Materials* series)

ANTOINE DE SAINT EXUPÉRY (1900–44)
FRANCE

THE LITTLE PRINCE (1943)

Antoine de Saint Exupéry learned to fly when he was a young man and his careers as aviator and author unfolded in tandem in the late 1920s and 1930s. Works like *Southern Mail* and *Night Flight* drew on his experiences as a pilot in both Europe and South America. *Wind, Sand and Stars*, first published on the eve of the Second World War, mixes philosophy and lyrical prose in its descriptions of flying on dangerous mail runs across the Sahara and some of the highest peaks in the Andes. Saint Exupéry's most famous work by far remains *The Little Prince*, written when he was living briefly in the USA in 1942 and published the following year. Superficially this is a simple children's tale about a pilot who crashes his plane in the Sahara and there meets a 'little prince', an extraterrestrial young boy from a tiny asteroid, who tells him of life on his own world and of his interplanetary travels. Yet, beneath the external trappings of the children's story, is a much more profound parable about human life. At its core is the belief that only by retaining a child's vision of the world can a person display true maturity, a truth that most adults have forgotten. 'It is only with the heart that one can see rightly,' the little prince says, 'what is essential is invisible to the eye.' Saint Exupéry went on to fight with the Free French forces during the war and was killed in 1944 when his aircraft crashed into the Mediterranean during a routine intelligence mission. His fable of the 'little prince', filled with wit and wisdom and fuelled by a gentle awareness of the power of love and innocence to transform our lives, continues to charm readers more than six decades after his death.

≋Read on
Night Flight; *Southern Mail*; *Wind, Sand and Stars*
Beryl Markham, ***West with the Night***; Consuelo de Saint Exupéry, ***The Tale of the Rose*** (memoir by Saint Exupéry's widow); Oscar Wilde, ***The Happy Prince and Other Stories***

J.D. SALINGER (b. 1919) USA

THE CATCHER IN THE RYE (1951)

Over the years, J.D. Salinger has become as famous for his reclusiveness as he has for the quality of his work. His published output consists of one novel and a handful of short stories. He has not allowed any new work to appear in print since 1965. Yet he remains one of the most acclaimed American writers of the last century. Much of his reputation rests on that one novel – *The Catcher in the Rye*. The book tells the story of troubled teenager Holden Caulfield who is about to be expelled from his boarding school. Appalled by the phoniness of the adult world, Holden runs away to New York and checks into a hotel where he begins to contemplate what the future holds for him. As he mooches about the city, struggling to make sense of life, himself and the opposite sex, he broods on possible courses of action. Should he hitchhike out west and start a new life away from everybody he knows? Should he lose his virginity and, if so, how? Told in Holden's distinctive voice, *The Catcher in the Rye* is a portrait of adolescent angst that strikes a chord with anyone who knows or remembers how confusing growing up can be. Holden has his own literary opinions. At one point in his story, he remarks that, 'What really knocks me out is a book, when you're all done reading it, you wished the author that wrote it was a terrific friend of yours and you could call him up on the phone whenever you felt like it.' Salinger's great achievement in *The Catcher in the Rye* – and it's as true now as it was when it was published – is that his novel reads exactly like the kind of book that Holden so admired.

See also: *100 Must-Read Books for Men*

⮒Read on
For Esmé with Love and Squalor; *Franny and Zooey*
Stephen Chbosky, *The Perks of Being a Wallflower*; F. Scott Fitzgerald, *The Great Gatsby*; Mark Twain, *The Adventures of Huckleberry Finn*

ERIC SCHLOSSER (b. 1959) USA

FAST FOOD NATION (2001)
Schlosser is an investigative journalist who, before his assault on the fast food industry, was best known for 'Reefer Madness', a long article on the contradictions and illogic of the USA's official policy on marijuana which was first published in *Atlantic Monthly*. *Fast Food Nation*, which began life a series of articles for *Rolling Stone*, is an unflinching exposé of what, in the words of its subtitle, 'the all-American meal is doing to the world'. The book is premised on the belief that, as Schlosser says, 'A nation's diet can be more revealing than its art or literature.' The claim might seem an exaggerated one but Schlosser has the statistics to back

it up. 'Americans,' he writes, 'now spend more money on fast food than on higher education, personal computers, computer software, or new cars. They spend more on fast food than on movies, books, magazines, newspapers, videos, and recorded music – combined.' If we assume that people spend most money on those things they most love, then Americans really love fast food. And both for America and the rest of the world the consequences of that love are often disastrous. For consumers the exponential expansion of fast food has meant a growing epidemic of obesity and all the health problems associated with it. As Schlosser points out, 'it seems wherever America's fast food chains go, waistlines inevitably start expanding'. For those in the production line of fast food, it has meant exploitation and poor working conditions. Because of the myriad methods by which marketing men in the industry target the young, all the problems associated with fast food are likely to grow worse rather than better unless we radically change our attitudes to consumption. Read *Fast Food Nation* and you will never look at food and eating in the same way again.

⮂Read on

Reefer Madness and Other Tales from the American Underground
Barbara Ehrenreich, *Nickel and Dimed*; Morgan Spurlock, *Don't Eat This Book*

E.F. SCHUMACHER (1911–77) GERMANY/UK

SMALL IS BEAUTIFUL (1973)

Ernst Schumacher was born in Germany but came to Britain before the Second World War to escape living under the Nazi regime of the 1930s. Briefly interned during the war, he worked on economic planning for the welfare state reforms instituted by Attlee's Labour government and then, for twenty years, as chief economic adviser to the National Coal Board. Steeped in the traditional ideas of economists, Schumacher was sufficient of an individual and a maverick to be able to think outside the box and to question some of the most basic assumptions of his peers. Perhaps the best summary of his philosophy can be found in the subtitle to his most famous book. *Small Is Beautiful* is 'a study of economics as if people mattered'. The central criticism he made of existing economic systems was not only that they ignored the real needs of real people but that all of them, especially western capitalism, encouraged an entirely unrealistic view of the world and its resources. 'An attitude to life which seeks fulfilment in the single-minded pursuit of wealth – in short, materialism – does not fit into this world,' he wrote, 'because it contains within itself no limiting principle, while the environment in which it is placed is strictly limited.' Schumacher went on to write other books, including *A Guide for the Perplexed* (once described as 'a statement of the philosophical underpinnings that inform *Small is Beautiful*'), but it is the earlier work that remains the most influential. Schumacher was a man ahead of his time – a remarkable intellectual pioneer of ecology, sustainable development and appropriate technology. As the decades pass and the threats of over-development and dwindling global resources grow, *Small is Beautiful* is likely to seem more and more prescient in its arguments.

⮂Read on

Good Work; *A Guide for the Perplexed*
J.K. Galbraith, *The Affluent Society*; D. Meadows et al, *Limits to Growth*; Barbara Wood Schumacher, *Small Is Still Beautiful*

ERNEST SHACKLETON (1874–1922) IRELAND

SOUTH (1919)

Shackleton is one of the great names from what is known, quite rightly, as the 'heroic age' of polar exploration. A member of Captain Scott's first expedition to the Antarctic, he organised his own attempt to reach the South Pole in the years 1907 to 1909 and came within 100 miles of reaching his goal before being obliged to turn back. His book *South* records his experiences and those of the men he led in the British Imperial Trans-Antarctic Expedition which left England a few years after Scott's doomed journey to the Pole. The aim of the expedition was to make the first land crossing of the Antarctic continent but Shackleton's ship, the *Endurance*, was trapped by the pack ice before reaching the intended landing point. His men were forced to abandon ship and, after months of drifting on ice floes, to take refuge on the desolate Elephant Island. Realising that there was no possibility of rescue otherwise, Shackleton and five others set off in a 7-metre-long lifeboat on an 800-

mile journey through frozen seas to South Georgia where the men living on remote whaling stations offered the hope of contact with civilisation. The boat came ashore on the opposite side of the island to the stations and Shackleton and his companions were obliged to make the first crossing of the mountainous South Georgia in order to reach them. Eventually, all the men left on Elephant Island were rescued. 'We had pierced the veneer of outside things,' Shackleton writes of what he and his men had endured. Later he adds, 'We had reached the naked soul of man.' As a record of the journey, both spiritual and physical, that the polar explorers made, *South* is an unforgettable narrative. It is one of the most harrowing and yet most uplifting of all stories of survival in a hostile environment.

⊜Read on

Apsley Cherry-Garrard, *The Worst Journey in the World*; Alfred Lansing, *Endurance: Shackleton's Incredible Voyage*; Robert Falcon Scott, *Journals: Scott's Last Expedition*

READONATHEME: EXPLORATION AND ENDURANCE

Richard Henry Dana, *Two Years Before the Mast*
Heinrich Harrer, *Seven Years in Tibet*
Sven Hedin, *My Life as an Explorer*
Thor Heyerdahl, *Kon-Tiki*

> Sebastian Junger, *The Perfect Storm*
> Mary Kingsley, *Travels in West Africa*
> Jon Krakauer, *Into Thin Air*
> Fridtjof Nansen, *Farthest North*
> Slavomir Rawicz, *The Long Walk*
> Piers Paul Read, *Alive*
> Joe Simpson, *Touching the Void*
> Wilfred Thesiger, *Arabian Sands*

CAROL SHIELDS (1935–2003) CANADA/USA

THE STONE DIARIES (1993)

Carol Shields was born in Illinois but she married a Canadian when she was in her early 20s and most of her adult life was spent in Canada where she taught English literature at universities and published a series of highly-acclaimed novels. Like Jane Austen, whom she admired greatly, she was a novelist with an ability to write about apparently ordinary people, leading lives that might be considered, from the outside, to be narrow and restricted, and yet to find within her characters elements of the extraordinary. Her finest novel is *The Stone Diaries* which is the story of an 'ordinary' woman's life from birth in rural Canada to her death in a Florida nursing home 90 years later. Daisy Goodwill Flett, as the chapter headings of the book (Birth,

Childhood, Marriage, Love etc) ironically underline, lives in one sense a conventional life as (in her son's words at her memorial service) 'wife, mother, citizen of our century'. In another sense her life is most unconventional, including elements that would not have looked out of place in a magic-realist novel. Her mother dies in childbirth without even realising she is pregnant. A neighbour returns to his native Orkney and lives to the age of 115, proud of his ability to recite *Jane Eyre* from memory. And the novel in which Daisy's life is told is far from conventional. It mimics the form of a non-fiction biography with family tree, photographs of family members, excerpts from letters, journals, newspaper articles and so on. In a poignant, knowing and funny narrative, Carol Shields carefully unfolds the remarkable story of a supposedly unremarkable woman. Once encountered on the pages of Shields's novel, Daisy Goodwill Flett is never forgotten. As one critic wrote at the time of the book's first publication, '*The Stone Diaries* reminds us again why literature matters'.

⟫Read on

Larry's Party; *Mary Swann*
Margaret Laurence, *The Stone Angel*; Anne Tyler, *Breathing Lessons*

PETER SINGER (b. 1946) AUSTRALIA

ANIMAL LIBERATION (1975)

What rights do non-human animals have? How far should we, as moral beings, consider these rights when we are making decisions which affect them? In 1975, the Australian philosopher Peter Singer published what has become, in many ways, the central text for the animal liberation movement. The book was called simply *Animal Liberation* and it condemned what Singer called 'the tyranny of human over non-human animals'. As Singer went on to say, it was (and is) intended for 'people who are concerned about ending oppression and exploitation wherever they occur, and in seeing that the basic moral principle of equal consideration of interests is not arbitrarily restricted to members of our own species.' If we believe that discrimination should not take place on the basis of race or sex, then it is logical to believe that we should not discriminate on the basis of species. Speciesism is as morally reprehensible as racism and sexism. Other species are sentient and as capable as us of suffering. As the utilitarian philosopher Jeremy Bentham said two centuries ago, 'The question is not, Can they reason?, nor, Can they talk? But, Can they suffer?' It is quite clear that animals can suffer and Singer spends a good part of *Animal Liberation* exposing just how we inflict pain on other species in two particular areas – animal experimentation and factory farming. Singer's book is so powerful because it is much more than a dry exercise in academic philosophy. He provides an intellectual underpinning for the animal rights' movement but he also provides an impassioned plea for a new morality and a practical agenda for changing our lives so that animals no longer suffer at our hands. The campaign against speciesism may well prove one of the more important movements of the twenty-first century and it is impossible to imagine it without the work of Peter Singer.

⮺Read on

The Ethics of What We Eat

Stephen L. Clark, *Animals and their Moral Standing*; Tom Regan, *The Case for Animal Rights*

ALEXANDER SOLZHENITSYN (1918–2008)
RUSSIA

ONE DAY IN THE LIFE OF IVAN DENISOVICH
(1962/1963)

In 1945, Alexander Solzhenitsyn was an artillery officer in the Red Army who had been twice decorated for bravery and dedication to duty when he made the mistake of criticising Stalin in a private letter. His criticism came to the notice of the authorities and he was sentenced to an eight-year term in a labour camp. After his release he worked as a maths teacher and began to write. The novella *One Day in the Life of Ivan Denisovich* first appeared in Russian in the literary magazine *Novy Mir* in 1962, reportedly only after Khrushchev had given his permission for it to do so, and it was published in an English translation the following year. The book does exactly what its title suggests. It chronicles one day in the life of an inmate of a Soviet prison camp. Ivan Denisovich

Shukhov feels ill when he awakes but he is none the less forced to undertake hard manual labour alongside his fellow prisoners. Through Shukhov's eyes, we see the everyday routine of the camp, the relentless obsession with food, the attempts by the inmates to gain some small advantages in the struggle for survival. With its simple, unadorned language and the obvious authenticity of its descriptions of life in the camps of the Gulag, the book caused a sensation both in the Soviet Union and abroad. Solzhenitsyn's period in official favour proved a short one. By the mid-sixties, his work was appearing only in samizdat publications and, in the mid-seventies, the writer went into an exile in the West that lasted twenty years. His later work was more epic in scale but, arguably, nothing Solzhenitsyn wrote subsequently had the same direct impact on readers as *One Day in the Life of Ivan Denisovich*. It is a short book but one that has much to say about human nature stripped to its basics.

⮒Read on
Cancer Ward; *The Gulag Archipelago*
Fyodor Dostoyevsky, *The House of the Dead*; Vasily Grossman, *Life and Fate*; Arthur Koestler, *Darkness at Noon*

ART SPIEGELMAN (b. 1948) SWEDEN/USA

MAUS (1972–91)

Once described by Alan Moore as 'perhaps the single most important comic creator working within the field', Art Spiegelman began his career on the proliferating underground 'comix' of the late 1960s and early 1970s. His greatest achievement has been to use the style and format of the comic book to tackle a subject that most people would have assumed to be beyond the reach of the genre – the Holocaust. Drawing on the recollections of his parents and their experiences as Polish Jews of Nazi persecution, Spiegelman spent nearly twenty years developing and refining the graphic work which, in effect, told their tale. *Maus* began its existence as a few strips in an underground comic and eventually became a long, two-volume masterpiece. In its final form, it chronicles the life of Vladek Spiegelman, Art's father, in various towns in south Poland during the late 1930s and the events which led him to Auschwitz but it also jumps forward in time and records the new life Vladek forged for himself and his family in New York. The characters in the comic are anthropomorphically portrayed as animals. Jews are mice, Germans are cats. Other creatures represent other nationalities. *Maus* has had its critics – some people are queasy with his use of animals to depict ethnic and national groups, feeling that it is uncomfortably close to the ways in which Jews were shown in Nazi propaganda – but it has proved an inspirational work of art to others. Spiegelman's intention was always to undermine racial and national sterotypes, rather than confirm them, and, for most readers, his satiric use of the comic convention of anthropomorphising animals in *Maus* does just that. His book ultimately transcends the genre in which it was created and becomes an immensely powerful and uplifting tale of persecution, suffering and survival.

⮂Read on

In the Shadow of No Towers (Spiegelman's response to the events of 9/11)

Will Eisner, *A Contract with God*; Joe Sacco, *Palestine*; Marjane Satrapi, *Persepolis*

HENRY DAVID THOREAU (1817–62) USA

WALDEN (1854)

In the 1840s, the American writer and intellectual Henry David Thoreau spent two years living alone in an isolated cabin in the woods of Massachusetts, growing his own food and attending to his own simple needs. Out of this experience came *Walden*. Few other works embody so well the American belief in individual freedom and the importance of self-sufficiency and ploughing one's own furrow in life. Thoreau's book is an extraordinary mixture of the visionary and the practical. He emphasises the quasi-religious properties of a communion with nature but he also describes his domestic economy, his agricultural experiments and his observations of flora and fauna with great precision. He questions the materialism of his age and the work ethic behind it yet he never loses sight of the 'real' world of civilisation to which he returned.

Combining philosophy, political thought and natural history in his writings, Thoreau can be seen as a forerunner of today's ecologists and environmentalists. Most of all, he remains an eloquent advocate of the importance of listening to one's inner voice. Sometimes doing so might lead one into difficulties, even into direct opposition to authority. Thoreau himself was very briefly imprisoned when he refused to pay his taxes because of his disapproval of slavery and of the Mexican-American war, a refusal he justified in a famous essay entitled 'Civil Disobedience'. Society for Thoreau was important but it was not so important as the freedom of the individual. In the final analysis, a man could not surrender to the wishes of the majority his own freedom to act as his own conscience and inner self told him he should. As Thoreau wrote in *Walden*, 'If a man does not keep pace with his companions, perhaps it is because he hears a different drummer. Let him step to the music which he hears, however measured or far away.'

⮃Read on

Civil Disobedience; *A Week on the Concord and Merrimack Rivers*
Edward Abbey, *Desert Solitaire*; Ralph Waldo Emerson, *Selected Essays*; Benjamin Franklin, *Autobiography*; Aldo Leopold, *A Sand County Almanac*; Norman Maclean, *A River Runs Through It*

J.R.R. TOLKIEN (1892–1973) UK

THE LORD OF THE RINGS (1954–55)

Born in South Africa but brought to England as a young child, Tolkien grew up to spend the greater part of his adult life as an academic. Only service in the First World War, in which he fought at the Somme, interrupted the even tenor of a life passed mostly in England's ancient universities and in the study of language, literature and mythology. The results of that study were not only academic works like the standard edition of the Middle English poem *Sir Gawain and the Green Knight* but also the vast, three-volume saga entitled *The Lord of the Rings*. Set in the fantasy lands of Middle-earth, and peopled by an array of men, hobbits, elves, dwarves, orcs and other races, *The Lord of the Rings* chronicles the struggle for possession of the One Ring and its powers and the ongoing confrontation between the forces of good and the forces of evil in Middle-earth. In the fifty years since the books appeared, many other authors have followed in his path and written epic works of fantasy but Tolkien outclasses all his imitators. He does so not so much because of his plot (the simple and morally explicit battle between good and evil is easy to replicate) as thanks to his teeming imagination. Drawing on his own encyclopaedic knowledge of such subjects as Norse mythology, Anglo-Saxon literature and medieval philology, he gave his made-up worlds complete systems of language, history, anthropology and geography. Reading him is like exploring an entire library – his invention seems inexhaustible. In poll after poll in recent years, Tolkien's masterwork has been chosen as the greatest and best loved novel of the twentieth century. There seems little reason to suppose that this verdict will change in any future public votes.

🕮**Read on**

The Silmarillion
Robert Jordan, *The Eye of the World* (the first in the epic 'Wheel of Time' series); Ursula Le Guin, *The Earthsea Quartet*

LEO TOLSTOY (1828–1910) RUSSIA

THE KINGDOM OF GOD IS WITHIN YOU (1894)

Tolstoy is, of course, best-known as a novelist and *War and Peace* and *Anna Karenina* are regarded by most critics as two of the greatest novels ever published. These two masterpieces are works of their writer's middle years. As he grew older Tolstoy became increasingly disenchanted with the books he had written and, indeed, with the whole notion of fiction. He was drawn into a profound moral struggle in which he began to look upon his life so far, and his earlier writings, as empty and meaningless. This spiritual crisis and Tolstoy's attempts to find answers to his questions about the meaning of life are chronicled in *A Confession*, written in the early 1880s. A dozen years later, Tolstoy published *The Kingdom of God is Within You*, a summation of the Christian ideas in which he came to believe. His ethical writings, including *The Kingdom of God Is Within You*, revolve around a belief in the overwhelming importance of love (towards both God and humanity) as a moral principle. Evil, in this view, was not to be directly resisted, private property was to be renounced and governments and churches, which stifled the soul, were to be abolished. Over the years, Tolstoy himself made over his fortune to his wife and increasingly took upon himself the dress and habits of the peasants he admired. His religious credo in his final years had little to do with established religions. 'Nowhere nor in anything, except in the assertion of the Church,' he wrote, 'can we find that God or Christ founded anything like what Churchmen understand by the Church.' Instead he found his spiritual salvation in what he saw as the uncorrupted truths expressed by Christ in the Gospels. Tolstoy's willingness to acknowledge the radical implications of Christian belief continues to challenge hypocrisy and complacency a century after his death.

See also: *100 Must-Read Classic Novels*

≋Read on
A Confession; *Resurrection* (Tolstoy's last major work of fiction deals with many of the same ideas and themes that can be found in his ethical writings)
Peter Kropotkin, *The Conquest of Bread*

LAO TZU (?6th century BC) CHINA

THE TAO TE CHING (?6th century BC)
In Chinese tradition, Lao Tzu is described as a contemporary of Confucius but more recently scholars have expressed doubts about his reality as a historical figure and have argued that the *Tao Te Ching*, the text ascribed to him, is an amalgamation of writings and sayings by a

number of individuals. Certainly some of the stories attached to Lao Tzu's name suggest a legendary hero rather than a historical character. He is variously said to have been born as a old man with a grey beard, after sixty-two years in the womb, to have lived for nine hundred and ninety years and to have owed his conception to his mother looking at a falling star. Whether Lao Tzu was a historical figure or a legendary one matters less than that the writings attributed to him have long had a central place in Chinese culture and that they continue to provide inspiration and meaning in the lives of millions of readers around the world today. Tao means literally 'way' or 'path' and the *Tao Te Ching*, at its simplest level, is a guide to how to live one's life virtuously and in harmony with the universe. The path, however, is not necessarily easy to pick out. The *Tao Te Ching* is an enigmatic guide. 'The Tao that can be told is not the eternal Tao,' it begins, 'The name that can be named is not the eternal name.' It becomes no simpler as its lines progress. Only by study and meditation on the paradoxes and ambiguities of the *Tao Te Ching* can its multiple meanings be understood. For those in search of an easy road to enlightenment, this classic of Chinese literature and philosophy is not recommended; for those prepared to work towards right living and right thinking, its subtleties repay regular reading.

≋Read on

Benjamin Hoff, *The Tao of Pooh*; Alan Watts, *Tao: The Watercourse Way*

READ ON A THEME: WISDOM FROM THE EAST

Confucius, *Analects*
The Gospel of Sri Ramakrishna
The I Ching
The Lotus Sutra
Paul Reps (ed), *Zen Flesh, Zen Bones*
D.T. Suzuki, *Essays in Zen Buddhism*
Alan Watts, *The Way of Zen*
Richard Wilhelm (ed), *The Secret of the Golden Flower*

SUN TZU (?544 BC–?496 BC) CHINA

THE ART OF WAR (?6th century BC)

The Art of War is the oldest and very probably the most influential of all books about military strategy. Probably written six centuries before the time of Christ, it was translated into French by a Jesuit priest in the eighteenth century but the first English version did not appear until 1905. Since its publication in the West, its value has always been recognised. Generals from Napoleon to Douglas MacArthur have drawn upon the wisdom it contains. Modern business leaders, politicians, chess players and football managers have all found the lessons it inculcates of value. Even fictional mafiosi find it of interest. In an episode of the TV series *The Sopranos*, Tony Soprano admits to a friend, 'Been reading that book you told me about. You know, *The Art of War* by Sun Tzu. I mean here's this guy, a Chinese general, wrote this thing 2400 years ago, and most of it still applies today!' Crime boss Soprano is speaking no more than the truth. Originally devised during a period of almost non-stop warfare between rival Chinese states, the ideas expressed in *The Art of War* have proved adaptable to changing circumstances over the ensuing centuries. Sun Tzu's theory of strategy, with its emphasis on self-knowledge and preparedness ('If you know others and know yourself, you will not be imperiled in a hundred battles'), can be almost endlessly re-interpreted and re-applied. The author of *The Art of War* was a near contemporary of Confucius but, like the great Chinese philosopher-statesman, his work still speaks to people living in societies utterly unlike the one in which it was written. It can offer insights on life to those who have never set foot on a battlefield and to those who are never likely to find themselves, like Tony Soprano, at the head of an organised crime family.

⮂Read on

Carl von Clausewitz, *On War*; Niccolo Machiavelli, *The Prince*; Miyamoto Musashi, *The Book of Five Rings*

KURT VONNEGUT (1922–2007) USA

SLAUGHTERHOUSE-FIVE (1969)

Kurt Vonnegut was born in Indiana and was studying at Cornell University when he enlisted in the US Army. Vonnegut's views of the world and of humanity were profoundly shaped by his experiences when he served in the American forces in Europe during World War Two. Captured by the Germans, he was present in Dresden in February 1945 when the city was firebombed by the Allies and tens of thousands lost their lives. Vonnegut survived but the bombing of the city scarred him for the rest of his life. In some sense, all his later writing can be seen as a response to the destruction of Dresden and as an attempt to explain his own chance survival but *Slaughterhouse-Five*, in particular, takes the facts of his life and transforms them into remarkable fiction. The central character in the novel is Billy Pilgrim whose experiences in World War Two echo those of Vonnegut. However, Billy is also a person who has become 'unstuck' in time. His life does not unfold for him in chronological order but moves randomly back and forth along its timeline. What is more, he is in contact with aliens from a planet named Trafalmadore. Indeed, he is at one point kidnapped by the Trafalmadorians who exhibit him in a zoo and expect him to mate with a porn actress. Nonetheless it is through his contact with the Trafalmadorians that Billy comes to terms with his life and gains some sense of peace. The aliens see the universe in four dimensions – the fourth being time – and thus know everything about their lives in advance. The result is a philosophy of acceptance and fatalism and, once Billy acknowledges the sense behind the apparent nonsense of the Trafalmadorian worldview, he can be happy. 'All time is all time,' the Trafalmadorians tell him. 'It does not change. It does not lend itself to warnings or explanations. It simply is.'

See also: *100 Must-Read Science Fiction Novels*

≋Read on
Cat's Cradle; *Galapagos*
Richard Brautigan, *In Watermelon Sugar*; Joseph Heller, *Catch-22*

ALICE WALKER (b. 1944) USA

THE COLOR PURPLE (1982)

Alice Walker was born in Georgia, the child of a poor farming family, and won college scholarships which provided opportunities to escape the poverty and limitations of her background. In the 1960s she became an activist in the Civil Rights movement and later worked as a journalist and editor. She has published many collections of her poetry and her fiction includes *The Third Life of Grange Copeland*, set in the rural Georgia in which she grew up, *Meridian*, the story of a young black woman active in the Civil Rights movement of the 1960s, and *Possessing the Secret of Joy*, a novel which explores the consequences of female circumcision, a practice which Walker has also outspokenly condemned in non-fiction writings. However, her most influential novel by far is *The Color Purple*, which won the Pulitzer Prize for fiction and was made into a big-budget Hollywood movie by Steven Spielberg in 1985. The book tells the story of Celie, a young black girl in the American Deep South, who suffers poverty, rape and the terrors of a violent marriage. Only when she meets the glamorous singer Shug Avery is she able to break out of the trap her life has become and find the love and fulfilment she has always been denied. Told through a series of diary entries and letters and notable for its eloquent use of black American vernacular, *The Color Purple* is a remarkable and inspiring book. Its title comes from a conversation between Celie and Shug about God. Shug says that she thinks, 'it pisses God off if you walk by the color purple in a field somewhere and don't notice it.' The novel traces Celie's journey from abuse and disempowerment to a position where she can celebrate not only 'the color purple' but all the other joys and riches of life.

⪢Read on

Meridian; *Possessing the Secret of Joy*
Zora Neale Hurston, *Their Eyes Were Watching God*; Toni Morrison, *The Bluest Eye*

EDMUND WHITE (b. 1940) USA

A BOY'S OWN STORY (1982)

Edmund White was born in Cincinatti and grew up in Chicago. After studying Chinese at the University of Michigan, he worked as a journalist and occasional novelist in New York before *A Boy's Own Story* became a critical and commercial success. In his fiction since then – in novels like *The Beautiful Room Is Empty* and *The Farewell Symphony* – White has charted the trajectory of a generation of gay men from the joyful promiscuity of the pre-AIDS era to the more sombre realities of lives overshadowed by the threat of death and disease. *A Boy's Own Story*, still his most famous book, works in a long tradition of the coming-of-age novel but re-imagines it from a gay perspective. Growing up in the America of the 1950s, a time of repression and suppression for gay men, White's nameless narrator has to struggle with his emotional isolation from his parents and his peers. His increasing awareness of his own homosexuality brings with it complicated feelings of desire and shame. Privileged because of his father's wealth and the material comforts it provides, his upbringing is also deprived. Both his parents are aloof and unloving and he yearns for an affection and an intimacy that are denied him. Only in the consolations of art and literature and in a sexual relationship with another, younger teenage boy, graphically but tenderly described in the novel, does he achieve some sense of what he is and what he might become. In an essay published in the early 1990s, White wrote that, 'As a young teenager I looked desperately for things to read that might excuse me or assure me I wasn't the only one, that might confirm an identity I was unhappily piecing together.' *A Boy's Own Story* has the power to do just that.

☙Read on

The Beautiful Room Is Empty; *The Farewell Symphony*
Alan Hollinghurst, *The Swimming Pool Library*; David Leavitt, *The Lost Language of Cranes*; Colm Tóibín, *The Story of the Night*

ELIE WIESEL (b. 1928) ROMANIA/USA

NIGHT (1960)

Elie Wiesel's life and work has been shaped by his experience of the Holocaust and by his own extraordinary determination to bear witness to the suffering he saw and to the attempted destruction of European Jewry by the Nazis. He was born into a Hasidic family in the Romanian town of Sighet and was a teenager when almost the entire Jewish population of the town was deported to Auschwitz. Wiesel survived his experiences in the concentration camp and on one of the so-called 'death marches' across Germany in the last months of the war but his parents and other members of his family did not. After the war he lived first in France where he studied at the Sorbonne and later worked as a journalist and then in the USA where he began to publish the fiction and non-fiction for which he is famous and to lecture on the Holocaust. For more than fifty years, Wiesel has been indefatigable in his efforts to ensure that the terrible experiences of millions of Jews at the hands of the Nazis should not be forgotten. He has been quoted as saying that, 'I decided to devote my life to telling the story because I felt that having survived I owe something to the dead ... and anyone who does not remember betrays them again.' *Night*, with its spare and undemonstrative narrative of the horrors that Wiesel saw as a scholarly and unworldly teenager brusquely thrust into the nightmare of Auschwitz, is a profoundly moving example of personal suffering transmuted into a work of art that speaks very directly to its readers. Most will agree with the statement made by the Nobel committee in 1986, when awarding him the Nobel

Peace Prize, that Wiesel is, 'a messenger to mankind; his message is one of peace, atonement and human dignity.'

⮂Read on

Dawn; *Day*; *The Forgotten*
Imre Kertesz, *Fateless*; Daniel Mendelsohn, *The Lost: A Search for Six of Six Million*

READONATHEME: SURVIVING THE HOLOCAUST (fiction and non-fiction)

Jean Améry, *At the Mind's Limits*
Aharon Appelfeld, *The Story of a Life*
Tadeusz Borowski, *This Way for the Gas, Ladies and Gentlemen*
Charlotte Delbo, *Auschwitz and After*
Fania Fénelon, *The Musicians of Auschwitz*
Gerda Weissman Klein, *All But My Life*
Olga Lengyel, *Five Chimneys*
Yehuda Nir, *The Lost Childhood*
André Schwarz-Bart, *The Last of the Just*

JEANETTE WINTERSON (b. 1959) UK

ORANGES ARE NOT THE ONLY FRUIT (1985)

Born in Manchester, Jeanette Winterson was adopted by an evangelical couple and brought up in the belief that she was intended by God to become a Christian missionary. In her teens she rebelled against this destiny, openly acknowledged her lesbianism and left home. After studying English at Oxford, she published *Oranges Are Not the Only Fruit* in 1985. In the years since then she has written a number of other novels ranging from works that mix elements of historical fiction and the magic realist novel (*The Passion* and *Sexing the Cherry*) to books like *The Powerbook* which play with ideas of time and cyberspace. She has also written fiction recently (*Tanglewreck* and *The Stone Gods*, for instance) aimed primarily at children. *Oranges Are Not the Only Fruit* clearly draws upon Winterson's own life. The central character, Jeanette, is adopted and, like her creator, grows up believing that she has a special destiny as a preacher and a missionary. She accepts this until, in her teens, she falls for another young woman and chooses love and sexuality over the demands of religion and family. However, there is much more going on in the book than simply a fictional remoulding of autobiographical experience. The novel is a rich celebration of diversity and difference. Very early on in the book Jeanette says of her mother, 'She had never heard of mixed feelings. There were friends and there were enemies.' The whole of the narrative stands as a rebuke to the black and white morality of Jeanette's mother. In the world that Jeanette chooses, it is mixed feelings rather than narrow certainties that are to be applauded. *Oranges Are Not the Only Fruit* is a novel that turns its back on small-mindedness and instead rejoices in the liberating power of love, sex, language and ideas.

☙Read on

The Passion; *The Powerbook*

Dorothy Allison, *Bastard Out of Carolina*; Sarah Waters, *Tipping the Velvet*

NAOMI WOLF (b. 1962) USA

THE BEAUTY MYTH (1991)

One of the so-called 'third wave' of feminist writers, Naomi Wolf shot to fame with her first book, *The Beauty Myth*, in which she argued that women were in thrall to false notions of beauty that merely served to keep men in the driving seat. '"Beauty", she wrote, 'is a currency system like the gold standard. Like any economy, it is determined by politics, and in the modern age in the West it is the last, best belief system that keeps male dominance intact.' Wolf's book is subtitled 'How Images of Beauty Are Used Against Women' and her argument is that the pressure on women to conform to a restrictive ideal of beauty serves to keep them under control. In 'the beauty myth' patriarchy has discovered a new means of keeping women in a subordinate position. Women, made insecure by the images presented in the media and in advertising, collaborate in the maintenance of this subordination but Wolf provides the ammunition in her book to destroy the beauty myth. In the years since the publication of *The Beauty Myth*, Wolf has continued to be a radical voice. Her most recent book, *The End of America*, raises her deep concerns that civil liberties are at risk in contemporary America and that the Bush administration has introduced and endorsed policies which have parallels in the rise to power of totalitarian regimes. However, none of her work has had quite the impact that her first book had. At a time when the number of anorexic and bulimic women is increasing, when cosmetic surgeons are finding that more and more women, dissatisfied with their own bodies, are willing to pay to go under the knife, when the diet industry makes billions worldwide, the message Wolf wished to convey in 1991 seems just as apposite in 2008.

≋Read on
Fire with Fire; *Promiscuities*
Susan Faludi, *Backlash*; Susie Orbach, *Fat Is a Feminist Issue*

VIRGINIA WOOLF (1882–1940) UK

A ROOM OF ONE'S OWN (1929)
The daughter of an eminent critic and scholar, Virginia Stephen was born into the heart of the intellectual establishment of Victorian England but, as a woman, was not given the opportunity to extend her education by attending university. Nonetheless, both before and after her marriage to the writer and political theorist Leonard Woolf, she was a leading member of the Bloomsbury Group, an informal association of

writers, artists and intellectuals which played a major role in British cultural life in the first few decades of the twentieth century. She is acknowledged as one of the most rewarding and innovative novelists of her time. In works like *Mrs. Dalloway*, *To the Lighthouse* and *The Waves* she revealed her fascination with individual psychology, using often avant-garde techniques of narration to reveal the internal lives of her characters. She was also a distinguished critic and author of non-fiction books that ranged from biographies to collections of literary essays. Despite all her achievements, she remained acutely aware of the limitations imposed on her by her sex. Based on a series of lectures Woolf gave at Cambridge University, *A Room of One's Own* is a witty, ironic but passionate plea for the liberty and personal space that artists, especially women, need to make the most of their imagination and creativity. Woolf draws on her skills as a novelist (she invents, for example, a sister for Shakespeare, one just as awesomely gifted as her brother, who finds that society offers her no opportunity to express her gifts) in order to express as vividly as possible her argument about the thwarting of talent and genius. Society has changed greatly over eighty years but its central thesis – that creativity demands freedom of many kinds – remains as true today as when *A Room of One's Own* was first published.

⊜Read on

The Common Reader; *Three Guineas*
Charlotte Perkins Gilman, *The Yellow Wallpaper*; Elaine Showalter, *The Female Malady*

PARAMAHANSA YOGANANDA (1893–1952)
INDIA

THE AUTOBIOGRAPHY OF A YOGI (1946)

Born in Uttar Pradesh, Paramahansa Yogananda became one of the first Indian spiritual teachers to live for long periods in the West and he introduced many westerners to eastern ideas about religion and meditation. His own teachings drew on a wide range of ancient traditions but his specific method was that of Kriya Yoga, a supposedly lost practice of yogic techniques revived by the mysterious Indian holy man Mahavatar Babaji. In *The Autobiography of a Yogi* Yogananda states that he received the teachings from his guru Swami Sri Yuktesar who had received them from his guru who had, in turn, been a disciple of Mahavatar Babaji. Whatever the origins of Kriya Yoga, it is at the heart of Yogananda's teachings, although its principles may not be the first things that readers remember about his book. At the simplest level, *The Autobiography of a Yogi* is just a great read. Its pages are filled with astonishing people (the Tiger Swami, who had wrestled and defeated tigers, the Levitating Saint, saints who have lived without food for decades), with miraculous healings and with events that defy the ideas of modern science. Yogananda's story, whether you believe everything that it contains or not, is very entertaining and written in an old-fashioned English that has charms of its own. Beneath the enjoyable telling of his tale, however, his message is clear. Man is a spiritual not a material being and it is the aim and the duty of each person to realise this truth. Yogananda's teaching can help in this process. 'The goal of yoga science,' he writes, 'is to calm the mind, that without distortion it may hear the infallible counsel of the Inner Voice.' Still the mind and the truth about our spiritual selves will be heard. It is a comforting and inspiring message.

≋Read on

Man's Eternal Quest

Sri Nisargadatta Maharaj, *I Am That*; Swami Sri Yukteswar, *The Holy Science*

GARY ZUKAV (b. 1942) USA

THE SEAT OF THE SOUL (1989)

Gary Zukav, Harvard graduate and Vietnam veteran, first came to the public's attention in the late 1970s as the writer of *The Dancing Wu Li Masters*, one of the best and most accessible of a number of popular science books published at the time which explored the similarities between quantum physics and Eastern philosophy. With *The Seat of the Soul*, published some ten years later, he switched his attention from science to the spiritual realm. In the book, Zukav questions the traditional, Western model of the soul with which most of us are familiar and proposes a new way of looking at spirituality. Everyone has a soul but, in Zukav's view, not everyone is aware of it. Some people remain mired in the realm of the senses and only when they can transcend the five senses and align their personalities with their multisensory souls will they reach their true potential. This new alignment is important not only for the individual but for the development of mankind in general. The changes which Zukav highlights are, he believes, all part and parcel of a new phase of human evolution. 'We are evolving,' he writes, 'from a species that pursues external power into a species that pursues authentic power. We are leaving behind exploration of the physical world as our sole means of evolution. This means of evolution, and the consciousness that results from an awareness that is limited to the five-sensory modality, are no longer adequate to what we must become.' Like Zukav's earlier book, *The Seat of the Soul*, with its attempt to join together elements of new age thinking, traditional religious belief and modern psychology, is an ambitious work. It may not always be successful but, for many of its readers, it provides a profound and inspiring journey into the world of the spirit.

⧉Read on

Soul to Soul

Deepak Chopra, *The Seven Spiritual Laws of Success*; Wayne Dyer, *Change Your Thoughts, Change Your Life*